T0193232

WOMEN WHO WALK THE TALK

*Experience the Freedom of
Authentic Self-Expression*

M.K. JONES

WOMEN WHO WALK THE TALK
Experience the Freedom of Authentic Self-Expression

The views expressed in this work are solely those of the author and do not necessarily reflect the views of the publisher, and the publisher hereby disclaims any responsibility for them.

iUniverse books may be ordered through booksellers or by contacting:

iUniverse
1663 Liberty Drive
Bloomington, IN 47403
www.iuniverse.com
1-800-Authors (1-800-288-4677)

Because of the dynamic nature of the Internet, any web addresses or links contained in this book may have changed since publication and may no longer be valid.

ISBN: 978-1-5320-8507-9 (sc)
ISBN: 978-1-5320-8508-6 (e)

Library of Congress Control Number: 2019915808

Print information available on the last page.

iUniverse rev. date: 10/29/2019

CONTENTS

INTRODUCTION

WHO IS A WOMAN WHO WALKS THE TALK?

E very woman alive has the potential to walk her own talk. In fact, each of us already walks our talk whenever we express our true self without apology or embarrassment. For many of us, this has proven extremely difficult, since we have been programmed since birth to act and talk in ways that are consistent with cultural norms and acceptable to others—including family, peers, and authority figures—though this reflexive approach isn't always in our best interests. The resulting pressure permeates our sense of selfhood until we can barely distinguish between our conscience and outside influence. Yet it's crucial to our well-being to love and believe in ourselves, to nurture our own growth, and to cultivate our self-confidence, so we can stand up for ourselves with respect for our uniqueness, find our personal passion, and realize our full potential, despite what may seem like undermining influences and overwhelming odds blocking our advancement.

As we each develop awareness of our astonishing capacity for good, we can begin to accept ourselves in all our complexity. We can:

- Forgive ourselves and others for actions and words that communicate a lack of compassion and lead to misunderstanding
- Express with effectiveness our deepest feelings of love and positivity
- Free ourselves from actions based on fear—replacing it with love
- Discover our highest values and true passions

- Believe in ourselves and our purpose to share our authentic expression
- Embrace our freedom while accepting responsibility for our actions
- Self-actualize: become our best selves and reach our full potential
- Experience the pure joy of authenticity
- Embody our most natural and healthy state of being
- Share our joy and love—our most natural state of being—with others

Becoming a woman who walks the talk is a lifetime process. It's a path toward authenticity and self-actualization. And it's a life-saving evolution toward truth and integrity. As we redeem our true selves we become more autonomous. We live by our own values as distinguished from others' limited perceptions of the women we are and the women we *ought* to become.

At the same time, we acquire the wisdom to honor human diversity and acknowledge our interdependence, reaching out to help and support one another in love and solidarity. And as we grow in numbers, telling our stories and sharing our concerns while we listen with empathy to both men's and women's voices, the world will become more enlightened, just, and humane. This thrilling adventure begins the moment we make the liberating choice to express our authentic selves and base our actions on our words.

FREEDOM

YOUR FREEDOM TO
COMMUNICATE

Most of us underestimate the potential power of our communication. When we become more aware of how our communication is impacting others in our lives we can make substantial progress in improving our skills and in turn humanizing our relationships.

Interpersonal communication involves at least two people. It's an interactive process. Even when it involves a leader, educator, or speaker, the audience is usually able to respond—at least in optimal situations. In the U.S., our Constitution provides for free speech in Amendment 1 as follows:

"Congress shall make no law respecting an establishment of religion, or prohibiting the free exercise thereof; or abridging the freedom of speech or of the press; or the right of the people peaceably to assemble, and to petition the government for a redress of grievances."

This comprehensive law entails communication that could even be considered one-sided, as in the media, such as radio, TV, and the written word. This gives everyone the right to speak freely, without censorship.

We also have the right to respond with our own points of view, regardless of whether they conflict with one stated by the press, a political party, or any group that claims authority over their doctrine or beliefs. Even our right to petition is protected.

These rights—considered privileges that people in other countries don't always share—charges our citizens with an inherent duty to follow our consciences in preserving our freedoms; it's part of the democratic process.

If we value our freedom and accept our responsibility in maintaining it, it's up to us to actively engage in any discussion, public or private, by standing up for our rights as individuals. This can apply to any forum: it can mean writing an editorial in reply to a news article or a letter to a TV network, or standing up to a bully in the neighborhood playground.

We have the right, but we also have the choice. We can choose to remain passive, and let the rest of our populace decide who will run the nation, or whether we'll have accessible healthcare, or affordable daycare, or equal pay for equal work. We're not forced to take an active part in a national discussion or a personal one. But in refusing to participate, we abdicate our power to use our influence for the betterment of society—including measures that will expedite women's advancement.

As a woman, it's critical that you understand you have a voice. It's your choice how you use it. Your unique voice is as vital to humanity as anyone's on the planet, as influential as you allow it to be, and as powerful as the courage it takes to express yourself, despite any forces that seem to stand in your way. Only you can empower yourself to defend your own rights, your own freedom, and the happiness you deserve.

Further, in responding to injustice you have another choice: you can respond with unrestrained hostility, or you can use your power for good, and contribute to solutions that will create a better world. Even when your anger is righteous and justified, it will only create hostile reactions if you limit your right to speak to using words of rage and despair. While rage may be an appropriate emotion and sometimes the most effective form of expression, it works best when we balance it with a composed and detached rationality.

Every time you communicate with the objective to accomplish acceptance and understanding, you're building a bridge with other human beings, whether they're in your geographic community or on the other side of the globe. But when you use words of hatred, you're *burning your bridge*—leaving only the ashes of destruction.

Believe in yourself as a force for good. The entire world needs to hear the powerful voice of reason, fairness, and dignity. Right now a large percent of that potential voice isn't heard—not with the strength and power that it's been created to project—and that's the voice of women everywhere!

YOUR FREEDOM TO LOVE

W hether we're female or male, and regardless of our sexual identity and preference, as we become more enlightened—learning to accept, forgive, love and believe in our imperfect selves—we naturally learn to extend our acceptance, forgiveness, love and trust toward others. This is a freeing process, since it releases the burdens of anger, hatred, and mistrust.

Resulting from our higher state of consciousness, we can no longer accept that some of us are lesser or inferior to others. We believe in the inherent equality of all mankind. We are all entitled to human dignity because we are all created as one. Ironically, when women use our voices to express the equality between men and women, we're labeled *feminists*. It seems a contradiction that a female would be considered a feminist, when we're advocating equality of the sexes rather than special privilege for women. Many of us are reluctant to accept the label, but insofar as the label is applied, women—and men—who are *feminist* support equality for both sexes.

An all-too-common misconception is that feminists hate men. This is a blatant untruth. Just as some men known to dislike or hate women are labeled misogynists, women who have an aversion to men are called *misandrists*. Being a misandrist is not one in the same as being a feminist. I suppose some misandrists could want gender equality and some misogynists could believe women's advancement would benefit both sexes. But to me this doesn't seem to be likely.

Feminists don't by definition hate men. Period. Exclamation mark! As a woman each of you is free to love, respect, and enjoy the men as well as the women in your life, regardless of his or her relationship to you. You don't need anyone's permission, or the green light from any movement claiming to champion women's rights. It's your right to decide for yourself how you feel about any particular man—or woman. But it's wise to limit any negative decision to one man or woman at a time, rather than condemn them all.

Further, men are not by definition the *enemy*—not in the abstract or in the flesh. No matter how ardent we are in wanting women's equality, it's not fair to hate men without qualification. It's generally conceded that men control over 90% of global wealth. This is patriarchy, and women have no reason to be happy about it. In fact, it's in everyone's best interest for us to advance in order to gain control over a more equitable portion of the currency pie, because it will immensely improve the global economy.

Besides, the act of hating an entire group is bigotry, whether it's hating all women or hating all men. Further, to assume all men or all women are alike is ignorant. It's stereotyping, and while most of us recognize this way of expressing prejudice in it's most flagrant form, some of us tend to voice *bias*, a more subtle and insidious practice, toward those of the opposite sex—sometimes *jokingly* or unwittingly—but with damaging results.

The fact is that it's not requisite that we hate anyone. As an emotion, it's an unnecessary weight on our shoulders—Neanderthal, ineffective, and further it makes us look stupid. At our best, we're too open-minded for hatred. It's just a matter of realizing we're free to love our fellow human beings without fear of judgment or reprisal. We can acknowledge that both men and women are wonderful, and not just when they're doing things our way. We can love them with all their flaws and failings, because they're human as we are. This doesn't mean we accept disrespectful or abusive behavior from anyone.

Yes, men are different from women in some ways, but isn't that part of the beauty of it all? Wouldn't it be a dull world if men thought and acted like us? *Vive la différence.* Life is so much more fun this way. Besides, in a world where women frankly need all the help we can get, it won't be until we acknowledge that men can be real life heroes and beloved superstars that they will be more inclined to accept roles as mentors, supporters, and teachers, not to mention partners and lovers. I can understand why men might be reluctant to share their power and wealth with venomous women who think they're no good. We create decent men's justified resentment when we flaunt our indiscriminate antagonism toward them.

It's OK to adore men and delight in their presence and it's OK to let them know it. The fact that the numbers show they have control of world's wealth doesn't in itself make them worthy of hate. It's really nothing personal. It only becomes personal when a man talks or acts in a way that demeans you, or expects something of you that compromises your values and makes you feel uncomfortable. Then you have a choice, a choice and a right to say "no." It doesn't require anger or hatred.

Your feelings toward men in this regard have little or nothing to do with your sexual orientation. No matter your sexual identity, men comprise about half of the human race. Since our population is diverse, in order to co-exist in relative peace it's beneficial for everyone that we get along with one another and divide our rights with equanimity and fairness.

Women are at liberty to love men without being subservient, meek, submissive, or passive because without exception we're their equals. And beneath their manly exteriors they love and need us, too.

In Front of Every Good Woman Is a Man

The familiar phrase *Behind every great man stands a woman* is considered dated and likely somewhat offensive—especially to women who advocate our advancement—but it's not quite obsolete. Although there's been progress, it's been more tedious than hoped.

Although today this idiom seems an obvious slam to the inherent equality of men and women, some women still appear to accept this assertion without recognizing the irony it holds. By reversing the quote's perspective to say *In front of very great woman stands a man*, basic truths about its intrinsic unfairness become evident that were all but buried in the original *Behind every great man stands a woman*.

The first is that we all have greatness within us, some of it unrealized, but the potential is always there. Our greatness doesn't depend on our heritage, our wealth, our personal assets, our accomplishments, or our gender. I believe our greatness—no matter our sexuality—lies within our strength of character and capacity for love. Millions of women are remarkable in our kindness and our level of integrity, although it often seems we have little or no opportunity to develop these powerful traits except perhaps in the home, if we are fortunate to have one. Sadly, millions more are left without homes at all, or homes that exhibit a lack of support that largely prohibits us in effect to work and earn enough to feed our families.

But whether we're destitute, under-served, or ostracized by

society or we're privileged, educated, and prepared with the tools we need for success, we all find men standing in front of us at pivotal points in our lives as well as in our day-to-day interactions. They may or may not be condescending to us, bullying us, or withholding their approval of our actions, but they still control the finances and make the rules, which maintain their one-up status.

Many of these men have more money and more power than we might ever expect to earn: It may be our fathers, our boyfriends, husbands, bosses, or the tradesmen who build and repair our houses and cars. Further removed but just as relevant, they include the men in government who might not find important our dire needs for childcare, medical services, protection from rape and abuse, equal pay for equal work, and other issues crucial to women. These men comprise the vast majority of our city, state, and federal representatives as compared to women, who hold a tiny percentage of positions in public office, just as male leaders at the top echelons of business are far more plentiful than their female counterparts.

The good news in the U.S. is that women are not only in a majority of the population, but for the first time in history, single women actually outnumber married ones. So why is it still so difficult for us to get laws enacted that will serve our best interests? Why don't more of us exercise our freedom to enter politics, or at least vote for those who advocate our rights?

Do the men who wield power intimidate us? Are we afraid of the consequences of becoming more assertive, even aggressive, in insisting our needs are met? Are we afraid of our own power, including the responsibility connected with standing on our own and reaching our potential, despite formidable male forces that we will no doubt confront? Is it still possible that some of us are complacent with our own creature comforts and don't care about defending women's rights along with our sisters who are fighting for fairness and a more inclusive economy? Are we blind to the urgency to solve issues of global poverty based on gender injustice?

Quite possibly, you're one of more than 76,000,000 women who have entered the work force. Or you're among the growing number of women entering politics and even running for office to advocate women's rights. If so, you would answer the questions in the previous paragraph with a resounding "No!"

Still, the reasons some of us hesitate to come forward may be understandable, considering our positions in life, which could be described as dependent, subjugate, and insecure at best. But if we are ever to advance to more financial independence—along with the freedom and empowerment it entails—we're compelled to devote our best effort to be the women who stand beside the men in our lives, not behind them. And we must own the fact that we're entitled to equal respect based on our shared humanity. We will find ourselves more than welcome to join the ranks of many women who are already working hard to make this vision a reality.

YOUR FREEDOM TO SUCCEED IN A MAN'S WORLD

As girls grow into women, it's imperative we feel confident that we're capable of self-reliance and that we have choices to be anything we wish to be as adults, if we're willing to do what it takes to achieve our goals. While we've advanced toward this end in recent decades, our circumstances are usually less than ideal as we reach adulthood. Self-doubt can emerge when a girl sees her brothers or the boys in school being encouraged to excel in sports, as well as math and science, while for her competitive pursuits are viewed as insignificant or *unfeminine*.

Peer pressure can arise when other girls seem more concerned about competing over a boy by looking her most attractive, rather than preparing for a career. Parental expectations take their toll if her mother coaches her to find a man to marry while she's still in school, so she can raise a family.

Some progressive thinking mothers urge and even inspire their daughters to follow their career ambitions, in spite of the fact that the playing field may be *shaky*—like the seismic waves of an earthquake. Perhaps mom has a career and has some idea of what her daughter can expect, or else she's never worked outside the home and her best hopes are based in an illusory concept of getting ahead in the workforce. Dad may be able to help. But only experience will teach the fine points of working in an environment where the cards are stacked against any woman on the brink of entering a profession or vocation which may be largely controlled by men.

Even if we're privileged enough to enjoy every advantage in attending the *right* schools and having the *best* connections, the tasks we set for ourselves in establishing financial independence can be monumental. While historically men have controlled a far greater percentage of wealth than women, the numbers are changing, but men still hold the vast majority of leadership roles and high-paying jobs in the U.S.

Clearly, young women need enough confidence to defy the odds against them, plus the unique skills required for their chosen occupations. Their ability to negotiate their value as employees in order to land positions equal to or above men is mandatory. The *Catch 22* is that to compete with men most women are required to learn these skills largely from the men with whom we're competing—those in control of most of the money and resources.

It's no small feat to enlist the help of the presumed rival. It requires tact and diplomacy. Plus we must convince men that we're a good investment—not just to make the world a *better place,* but to increase the bottom line; that is, make a profit—the motivation behind competition.

For centuries, men have depended on money to support themselves and their families. They're not going to risk losing it if they can avoid it.

Let's say a particular woman has outstanding qualifications on her resumé. In a perfect world in which everyone is totally honest and fair, she may be given a chance to hold a leadership role in a sector of business, law or medicine. She may be hired simply based on merit. On the other hand, in the real world, some individuals will do just about anything—whether or not it's ethical—to gain money and power. If an unscrupulous man—or woman—already has it, he or she will likely do what it takes to keep it, no matter whether it hurts another's career and earning potential.

Every woman who's considering entry into today's job market should be prepared for the competition and possible sabotage she will be forced to withstand when she attempts to move forward. She will need relevant training, not just a textbook education on the basics of her chosen field. A woman with courage, ambition and a thick skin can advance in the workplace, but she'll only find a real opportunity to triumph with her eyes wide open. As if this isn't enough, she needs the people skills to elicit others' support instead of making enemies if she's to have a chance to prevail. Women who advance in their work deserve our commendation and even our awe for their efforts toward financial independence. Regardless of how high a woman climbs on the *ladder to success* in her chosen endeavor, she deserves our respect for her fortitude and persistence.

I urge both men and women to be generous in reaching out to women who want to be self-sufficient in creating wealth that benefits the economy as a whole. A prerequisite for economic prosperity or perhaps survival today requires close to 100% participation of any population—a team of about 50% men and 50% women—to contribute the best of our talent, skill and integrity.

AUTHENTICITY

THE TRANSFORMATIVE POWER OF AUTHENTICITY

Each woman is a unique individual. And we each have a distinctive gift of genius that we were born to actualize. This should be a joyous process, but while we're all entitled to discover our authentic selves on a journey toward empowerment, we're likely to be distracted, frustrated, and intimidated along the way. Often we feel undermined in our quest for selfhood, validity, and our ability to do more, earn more, and be more according to our unique talents and skills,

Because I respect your humanity and uniqueness, I don't want to tell you what to think or how to feel. But I do want to help you discover how to think for yourself in a way that honors your authenticity, which is crucial for the self-sufficiency you crave. Becoming authentic is a lifelong journey that's both delightful and worthwhile, because it frees you from everything that's false and limiting in creating your highest self.

The concept of authenticity has two aspects that are aligned with one another: 1) our relationship with ourselves and 2) our relationship with others. We're out of alignment when we seek approval from others, yet never seem to receive it to our satisfaction; so we call ourselves *stupid*, *bad*, or any label that condemns us instead of seeing both our achievements and mistakes as experiences that lead us closer to our real selves.

When we communicate to ourselves that we're not worthy or that we're not *enough*, we are our own worst enemy. If someone else talked to us like we often talk to ourselves, we wouldn't want that person for a friend for very long. So why do we do this? The truth is, at a deep authentic level beyond all external judgments, we are more than enough. All of the negative input that we accept as accurate form obstacles to our self-realization: Some of our self-doubt may be in our DNA, or it might be from traumatic events that happened in the past or criticism from others, especially when we were young and impressionable. The damage is reinforced in adulthood, since we're programmed to expect it, and the hurtful cycle continues unless we consciously act to stop it from interfering with our potential for joy.

Our relationship with ourselves is most critical to our happiness. Besides, it's the fundamental basis of our effective or ineffective relationship with others. None of us is perfect: authenticity is not about always being positive and agreeable, and it's not about ignoring our anger. It's about being honest with ourselves and other people in our lives from an accepting, compassionate, and forgiving place in our hearts and minds.

Authenticity is our healthiest and most natural state of mind. Practicing authenticity is liberating, releasing us from the burden of disempowering influences. While it can without a doubt lead us to more of all the desirable things in life, these *things* don't matter if they're not meaningful to us. It's essential that we establish our own values and live by them. When we do this, I guarantee we'll find the joy of self-validation.

SELF-EXPRESSION AND AUTHENTICITY

Communication is infinitely more than the practice of putting words together. And it's a great deal more fascinating in its complexity: It's not just what we say, it's how we say it, and even more important what we do. Every blink of an eye and each of our movements communicates something very particular. Even if no one else is around, we communicate our words and actions to ourselves.

Almost anyone can learn to communicate effectively by 1) showing knowledge of what he or she is talking about, 2) using articulate language, and 3) stating his or her needs, desires, argument or point of view in a forthright, reasonable and persuasive manner.

An actor can convincingly communicate the thoughts and feelings of the character he or she is portraying, while at the same time thinking and feeling something entirely different. In everyday life as well, we tend to hide our true feeling and actual perceptions under a sort of communication *cover up*. We may rationalize that we're using good manners, or we don't want to hurt someone's feelings, and this is justifiable to an extent. But often the real reason we're not being honest is because we're uncertain and afraid of how others might react. We may be embarrassed or ashamed to tell our truth and face ridicule or rejection.

We involuntarily communicate clues that our spoken words are not really coming from our authentic selves. Some of the not-so-subtle red flags are 1) a disinterested tone of voice, 2) a prolonged sigh, 3) a pause, 4) eye movement, especially down and to the left, 5) body posture, such as slumping. This is just a partial list.

Nuance alludes to the more subtle cues regarding the relationship of our words and actions. Often without our consciousness, it can reveal we're not being our real selves. Like it or not, the human species has evolved into becoming quite astute in interpreting nuance. Women are often known to be perceptive in reading someone's feelings from the nuance in his or her communication.

When you're talking, your listener has an advantage: With more accuracy than you may imagine, he or she can observe that the words coming out of your mouth don't appear to be in *sync* with who you are or what's going on inside you. This disconnect doesn't occur when you express your authentic self, which is why it's so important that you understand, appreciate, and manifest the unique and powerful woman you have become.

You can start at this moment to get to know who you really are by questioning the limiting thoughts that you've allowed to be part of your ongoing internal dialogue. You can observe your communication patterns, which may be based on unthinking habits or false assumptions. And you can begin to practice projecting more confidence in your ability to relate to others with honesty, openness and positivity.

Communication is always most effective when it's based on genuine self-expression, a creative action that emanates from your true self. The term self-expression is often associated with the arts, including painting, music, and literature. When you express your real self in any endeavor, you raise your level of communication beyond just a skill and more to the level of an art form—an exciting and illuminating process of using your self-awareness to make meaningful human connection!

AUTHENTICITY IS PRICELESS

I want to share some really great news with you that you may not have thought of before in quite the same light. Understanding it now could change your life forever—empowering you as you never thought possible: It's the fact that authenticity has unlimited value. This may sound simple, but when you think of the ramifications of its value your appreciation can expand.

If we imagine a beautiful vase from antiquity that's been valued as *priceless,* we're aware the value of that vase is based on it authenticity. Because it's been determined that it comes from a specific part of the globe at a certain time, we can establish that it's genuine, not an imitation. This vase becomes priceless when it's the only one in existence. It has certain properties that cannot be duplicated, although some may try to copy it. The same is true of a painting or other object d'art that has *provenance*; in other words its origins can be traced to a particular artist, and it's documented to be one of a kind. Such paintings have been sold for hundreds of millions of dollars. Further, if something priceless is destroyed, it's considered a great loss, because it's irreplaceable.

If paintings and vases can be considered priceless, then certainly we can apply at least the same value to human beings. Each of us is unique: No one else is exactly like us. So already each of us is priceless. We're a miracle of the universe, created to perfection. As individuals, we are born exactly as we were meant to be. So we can use *priceless* as our starting point and experience the joy of increasing our value as we learn to access and develop our inherent authenticity. Sounds pretty good, doesn't it? It's more than good; it's fantastic!

Authenticity, when applied to the human species, is a word that means *honest, genuine, truthful*, and *trustworthy*. Its synonyms are *legitimacy* and *credibility*. These qualities in a person have enormous value, and to the extent we personify them our value becomes even greater.

This means that the more you can reach deep into your most authentic being and express your true self, the more valuable you are, and the more priceless your contribution to those around you—not only your family, friends, employers, teacher and other authority figures, but also total strangers, potential enemies—anyone and everyone who could benefit from your input, including the human race.

I don't believe most of you who are reading this are reacting with cynicism, thinking *good guys finish last* or honesty is for chumps, but if these thoughts have crossed your mind, think again. Yes, total honesty may be rare, but just like the work of art that's considered a *tour de force*, its relative scarcity makes it more valuable!

You're only truly original when you're being yourself. Otherwise, your persona is easily copied. So it's to your benefit to be honest first of all with yourself and then with others. Your relationship with yourself determines your self-respect, which is most important to your self-concept whether others believe in you or not. Another's perception of you depends largely on the self-respect you project, as well as your apparent honesty—as revealed by your nuance, body language and actions. When you become more credible, you increase your value to others, even beyond price. And as you evolve into expressing your best self, your worth begins to soar.

This is not to suggest that we each become wealthy or famous through the process of becoming ourselves, although it's entirely possible. It's just not necessary to our happiness and fulfillment. Even if no one believes us, recognizes us, or validates us during our lifetime, why should we waste one precious moment of our time trying to emulate others in order to be accepted, especially if it means compromising our values?

AUTHENTICITY ENHANCES
YOUR HEALTH

Being your true self is your most natural state of being and your healthiest approach to life. Just like fruit, veggies, and protein along with daily exercise can enhance your life experience and make you more immune to illness, so authenticity can greatly improve your overall health and levels of resilience when you practice it with consistency.

In everyday life—which somehow stretches into years and even decades—pretending you're OK when you're unhappy can contribute to chronic health problems. It's important to understand that it's likely to be less stressful to be authentic than to perpetuate an untruth. Stress has been repeatedly linked to poor health. In recent years, women have been shown to have a greater rate of heart attacks, which can be related to stress. Stress has markedly been connected to depression, anxiety and obesity in women.

Often we hide our feelings of anger, sadness, shame, or inadequacy for reasons we think are necessary to our survival. Perhaps we endure our boss's harassment to keep the jobs we urgently need to feed our families. Or, presumably to protect our children from the pain of a marital separation, we remain with a mate who neglects us. While our reasoning may reflect some validity and considerable unselfishness, our silent suffering is self-destructive behavior that can adversely affect our health.

On the other hand, when we pay attention to our authentic selves and treat ourselves with love and respect, we become more proactive in seeing that our essential needs—including enough rest and other forms self-care—are met with consistency. This is not merely a luxury. It's critical to our survival and that of our loved ones. Our good physical health and a positive state of mind are crucial before we can serve others with any success.

Many women desperately need more emotional support, financial opportunities, and possibilities for advancement. But before we can acquire these vital enhancements to our quality of life, it's essential that we learn to love and thereby empower ourselves. No one else will do it for us. Our progress begins when we learn to take care of our unique needs, so we have the strength to share our love with those we care about.

Today, the situation is far from hopeless. New initiatives are devoting amazing efforts to women's health and wellbeing through education and proper medical care. It's an exciting time to be part of this humanitarian movement toward women's need for improved financial welfare, more comprehensive health and safety measures, and more opportunities for substantial advancement.

If the concept of helping other women resonates with you, be assured the world ardently needs your compassionate influence. And if you haven't already joined the global alliance to empower women to create a more just and caring world, I believe you'll find engagement with other like-minded women and men exciting. Moreover, doing work that's meaningful to you as you help make the world a better place can be a profound pleasure. You can start by taking better care of yourself today, in small ways at first. Your productive steps toward better health—both mental and physical—will soon become habits that you will assimilate into your authentic approach to life.

AUTHENTICITY EMBRACES CREATIVITY

Authenticity honors your creativity since it's based on the premise that you are unique. Your individuality holds inestimable value when you embrace honesty and integrity in your words and actions—especially when you share it through creative self-expression.

Authenticity is making the choice to be truthful on a consistent basis. It requires the courage to be your real self in your relationships. At the same time, it's important that you're aware that being authentic isn't about violating your own boundaries or sense of privacy, or betraying your dignity, which are self-defeating ways of compromising yourself.

When you're looking deep within and being truthful with yourself, one variable you can't ignore is time, which necessitates change, as you can readily see in nature, where everything continually grows and evolves. Sometimes there's apparent destruction, but then life begins again. The most natural and healthy state of your mind is to be constantly learning and developing. You can try to stop or ignore this process, as many do, out of fear or discomfort that change will bring you pain, but change can be exhilarating and refreshing when you approach it with confidence.

We disregard change when we restrict ourselves to responding to outside stimuli in consistent ways that we assume are correct because that's been our habitual pattern. Our repetitive behavior places a needless burden on us to maintain some stagnant concept of rectitude or perfection that's impossible to achieve. Plus, it ignores the fact that we're intricate human beings with constantly changing needs.

As we become more self-aware, we want to express our best selves, which reflects a process of discovery that evolves over time. We actually have a delightful opportunity to continually recreate ourselves with each choice we make. Doesn't this sound a lot more rewarding than struggling to adhere to outdated standards with little or no relevance in our current lives?

Since authenticity is based on our uniqueness, which ideally evolves with the passing of time, it requires thinking *out of the box*. And it absolutely demands a mind open to new perspectives and ideas. It's all about creating new concepts, breaking new ground, and exploring new realities.

Real creativity is self-expression at its best. It's using our imaginations to bring new concepts into reality. As young children, self-expression is a natural occurrence: Unless we've endured severe trauma, we're usually confident and uninhibited in creating our *art* or *inventions,* with little or no thought about established standards of accuracy or correctness. But as we grow older, we often seem to lose much of our self-assurance and become painfully conscious of the opinions of others.

This pattern tends to repeat itself as we continue into adulthood. Instead of prizing our individuality, we suppress our creative instincts, most likely because we don't want to be seen as foolish, weird, or different from others. This fear is counterproductive. Often our difference is actually the source of our unique creative strength— our genius, if you will.

When you open your mind to your unique creativity, magic happens, especially if you allow yourself enjoyment in your exploration. Creativity is permitting your imagination to play. When you set your creative mind free, you're unrestricted in having the time of your life!

HOW TO BE A CREATIVE FORCE

I n our experience as women, there's never a shortage of advice and direction about how we should behave. Beyond this, the recommended behaviors center on presumed goals that we're expected to prioritize based on *appropriate* or *acceptable* standards. These imposed values may be regarding lifestyles, marriage, or whether or not to have children and/or careers. Or on a smaller and more trivial level, they can invade our personal preferences concerning how we look, what we eat, what we wear...the list is endless. Trying to adhere to current norms in order to be considered worthy of approval can be daunting and downright exhausting.

The questions become: 1) Whose consent are we seeking? and 2) Why are we placing more importance on another's approval than our own autonomy and self-esteem? There's not a single valid reason to put someone else's values and objectives above our own if we are self-sufficient adults. In fact, perhaps the most exquisite and enjoyable aspect of our personal freedom is our right to live a life that we continually create for ourselves, based on our unique desires.

Once you discover the joy of creating the life you want on every level, your awareness of all the possibilities that are open to you expands. Even better, it can never shrink back to that helpless feeling that you don't have choices. The most dangerous phrase in the world is, "We've always done it that way," which leaves no room for creativity, including the growth and learning that occur when you use its limitless power.

A sister to creativity is curiosity. An enjoyable aspect of doing things creatively is the results are at least in part a surprise. A creative approach to life requires the spirit of adventure and this can demand courage. It's good to know that the more you confront your unfounded fears with the love that engenders courage, the more it grows. It's all part of the fun.

You create a momentum when you consistently practice using your imagination, which can increase in power exponentially over time. Your creative actions—combined with love, courage, and positivity—actually create *vibes* that attract other like vibrations, as opposed to lower tremors of negativity and fear. Whether or not you believe in the Law of Attraction, it's a fact that energy begets more energy. By all means, don't wait to find out what the crowd is doing. Create your own reality. Take action! Therein lies adventure and excitement.

There's nothing wrong with being a rebel, especially when you're rebelling against something that doesn't feel right to you. Besides, doing things that others don't expect of you has its rewards. For one thing, it discourages others from taking you for granted. While I'm not advising you to do things out of spite, I am suggesting that you have enough self-regard to listen to your conscience and follow your own instincts.

When you live a life brimming with creativity, you'll never be bored. If you become restless, you can change things up—a little or a lot. This can mean something delicious and satisfying like creating a new recipe; or artistic, such as painting an abstract; or something as consequential as moving to a new city or launching a new business. If you become tired or fatigued, learn to rest as needed but don't give up on your passion unless it's no longer serving you.

Creative people are known to be experimental. They have a high tolerance for trial and error, which means they're usually not judgmental or smug. Instead they welcome open-mindedness, constructive ideas and progress. If this sounds like the person you are or the person you'd like to be, creativity is bottled up inside you that needs your full expression.

Time is precious. You don't need anyone's consent to do what's right for you. Go out there and create the life you want. Set your own objectives and be 100% accountable for meeting them. Then notice your capacity for pleasure and self-esteem rise off those limiting *charts* devised to measure your success. Don't hesitate a moment to begin.

Authenticity is Liberating

When you have an authentic approach to life, each moment of every day presents a new opportunity for positive change, personal growth and best of all becoming who you want to be.

Authenticity represents who you are now, not who you were or what you did or said in the past. It doesn't depend on who your parents were, how much money you have, or anything you may have done that has caused you to feel regret, embarrassment, or shame.

Many of us feel strapped in a mistake we made or something we said in haste, and this can't always be ignored; but we can reconcile it with what we've learned and how it's changed us to become who we are. We can forgive ourselves, stop judging others, and welcome the future. We will no longer feel compelled to blame our families or even our former enemies, who were in effect our teachers. We're not looking toward the past for validation or legitimacy, because we're too busy moving forward and enjoying life on our terms.

In your journey of self-discovery you may realize that an old way of doing things no longer serves you. You can find joy in accepting inevitable change and learning to let go. Even more freeing, you can be an active part in effecting that change instead of remaining a passive victim.

Sometimes you can find yourself in circumstances where you know you're perceived as *different*. This is not a cue to try to be like everyone else. There's beauty in diversity. If those around you can't accept this and insist through their words and actions that you should follow their example, it's probably time to make the change that will free you from their negative judgment, which is toxic in creating stress and attendant health issues.

In achieving authenticity you only compete with yourself out of a genuine aspiration to grow and self-actualize. As you focus on this objective, you don't find it necessary to compare yourself with others, who are on their own unique journeys. Your own evolution is more meaningful and pleasurable in achieving happiness and self-respect than remaining stagnant and settling for less than you desire. We all have the potential to find the joy of authenticity. It's not limited to any particular segment of humanity.

As women it's time we all make a conscious choice to offer one another the same support, encouragement and love that we ourselves crave in order to find the courage to express our authentic selves. It's been said, "Girls compete with each other, while women empower one another." Beyond this, I look forward to the day when both men and women are enlightened by the power of love and view one another as equal partners in advancing the human race toward understanding, compassion, and peace.

SELF-AWARENESS

SELF-AWARENESS CLARIFIES
YOUR VALUES

S elf-awareness is not just *navel gazing*—letting your mind wander and indulging in random thoughts about yourself— though let's not rule it out. It could be helpful in finding some direction in focusing on who you are.

The purpose of self-awareness and the source of its joy is in determining your core values, those that are most significant to you as a unique individual. In other words, you sort out the clutter and decide what you want in life.

Your values are yours alone. It in fact diminishes you to depend on anyone else for approval. No one can tell you what you should value. As a guide in helping you realize what will make you most happy and fulfilled, it's imperative you think for yourself regarding what's most important to you. Self-awareness is a self-empowering process.

What do you value most? You can begin to think about this anytime and anywhere, but since life is filled with distractions, I suggest you take some time alone, go to a private place—ideally one that's pleasant and peaceful— and let yourself relax, gently allowing thoughts about what you love come into your consciousness. Since your mind is now open to possibilities, this process is something like daydreaming.

The most effective way to decide what you value most may be to ask yourself, "What is my passion?" This is a key question, since what you most love will determine by what means you will become your true self.

While you might not think you have a passion, you can still ask yourself some related questions, such as:

- What activity do I most enjoy?
- What makes me happy?
- What is my special talent or skill?
- What do I find the most fun?
- What holds my attention?
- What challenges me to improve?

Go ahead, take a few minutes to ask these questions now and jot the answers down. Even if your responses seem disconnected at first, or even silly, when you start to look deeper, you may find a relationship between them that's unique to you. This in turn could lead to your discovery of your individual brilliance.

No matter how busy you are, the process of becoming more self-aware deserves your time and full attention. What could be more important than awareness of what you value most, which is that which will bring you joy?

FROM SELF-AWARENESS TO SELF-ACTUALIZATION

During the process of becoming more self-aware, you can progress from 1) realizing your values to 2) deciding who you are and 3) determining what you want to do with your life—at least at this point in time. Remember that things continually change and it's paramount to your future advancement that you remain flexible, open-minded and honest. You're free to reach your own conclusions, despite any undue influence from your families and friends. Although they may have your best interests in mind, they're not walking your journey or seeing things through your eyes, so they're not nearly as qualified as you are to know what's best for you.

Further, you would be wise to ignore negative comments from unsupportive peers who are likely unenlightened, stuck in a static place, cynical, or envious of your efforts to find meaning and happiness.

We are all *enough* just as we are, though a purposeful life inherently requires change and growth. While we can change without growth, it's impossible to experience growth without change. A healthy curiosity and a desire to learn are life-affirming traits. It's our most natural state of being to grow into the person we want to be and it all begins with the first step.

While you may already be content with your life when you set out to establish your goals, you'll benefit most if your mind is accessible to new ideas and perspectives. The first step towards getting somewhere is to decide you're not going to stay where you are. This doesn't necessarily suggest dissatisfaction with your current situation or position in life, although it's a valid reason for change. While you may be reasonably content, once you accept the inevitability of change, you're prepared to be proactive in identifying and preventing potential problems. In other words, you can take charge of your life—expanding your thoughts to include the ways that change can work in your favor.

If you're discontent with your life as it is now, becoming self-aware allows you to examine why you feel unhappy, unsatisfied, and restless for change. People often feel this way when they've outgrown their current circumstances. When a lobster outgrows its shell, it breaks free and grows a new better fitting one. So with human beings, if we are to continually evolve, we must cast off restraints that are no longer useful to us.

Our feelings may entail some degree of anger toward whatever or whoever seems to be holding us back. Anger can actually be a motivating factor in deciding our values. For example, as women we might feel anger toward a culture that allows discrimination. In particular, we might be angry with a boss who harasses us. This anger can consume us if we remain subservient to anyone who bullies us or makes us feel inadequate—even if we pretend things are OK. It's only when we take positive action and set achievable goals toward improving our situations that we begin to free ourselves from the toxic hold of others' attempts to control us to their advantage, as well as our own reluctance to change, which stems from our fear of the unknown.

To reach your core values in creating your goals, change your negative thoughts into positive ideas. In others words, become part of the solution, rather than a victim or a passive part of the problem. For example, instead of accepting your work life as hopeless, think about constructive ways to 1) find a better job; 2) become an entrepreneur; and/or 3) launch a nonprofit business to help advance a worthwhile cause. Self-awareness is an amazing process of realizing that you can make your dreams reality, but only if you're willing to do what it takes to make them come true. This can't be accomplished overnight.

Start to do what you can each moment toward accomplishing viable goals and thereby moving toward your objectives.

Self-awareness is the means to finding fulfillment. Deciding to venture on your unique path to a happy and meaningful life requires self-motivation, which will drive your actions and provide the self-discipline to achieve your goals. No one can do this for you. Ultimately, it's essential that you empower yourself to move forward in life.

YOU HAVE THE COURAGE
TO BE YOU

In the context of self-awareness, the will to change can involve 1) a major life change, such as a change of career, relationship, or lifestyle; 2) a change to a more effective approach to your work, relationships, or community; or 3) a change in your self-image and attitude toward others. Since these distinctions are intricately linked, you may end up making changes in all three categories.

It takes daring and resolution to make choices that reflect your ideal of what constitutes a successful life, often despite the opposing views of families, peers, or superiors. As your self-awareness enables you to evolve into a more authentic human being, ideally you begin to consider making choices that could have a positive impact on your fellow man. Your concern for others' wellbeing is totally different than allowing other people to make your choices for you.

When you're contemplating a change that you believe will improve your life because it reflects your real values, be prepared to experience some change in your relationships. Family members, friends, or even the most casual acquaintances may not readily understand or support your new direction. That's OK. Don't let it discourage you. The important thing to remember is that while you can't control others, you're in control of how you respond to their comments or criticism. Don't feel compelled to get defensive or angry at their lack of apparent interest or empathy. Instead, project a confident, courageous, and positive attitude regarding your choice. As long as you're not deliberately hurting someone with your behavior, you have a right to ownership of your decisions.

You'll have a better chance of satisfying your commitment toward a goal if the changes required to meet that goal are based on something that you can get excited about for an extended length of time. If you're going to be devoting all your time and energy to a particular action or outcome you want it to be something you enjoy. It will be a pleasure to pursue your objective with passion and enthusiasm. Otherwise, it could be extremely difficult to maintain your dedication, especially when the going gets tough.

Challenge is another motivating factor in making and sustaining positive change. If something doesn't challenge you, it won't have the power to change you. Although you might start with small steps in your first new endeavor, there's no point continuing to make easy choices to avoid possible failure. Challenge helps to build momentum in your chosen direction.

You may fear letting go of the familiar because you think it's more secure than the unknown. It's painful to hang on to what no longer has meaning in your life. But with passion, you can make the change that will lead you to self-reliance and joy. If you focus on the result that will meet your real desires and do what it takes to achieve it, you discover it's more than worth any temporary discomfort. Besides, there's great satisfaction in knowing you're beginning an adventure that will make you more resilient and ready to adapt to future changes that are bound to occur.

SELF-AWARENESS AWAKENS COMPASSION

Becoming self-aware is looking deep into our thoughts and emotions with honesty and objectivity. Before we're ready to move into the future and leave the past behind, it's advantageous to resolve any conflict and turmoil lurking in our memories. But where do we begin?

In understanding human beings, the findings of science and studies of spirituality are essentially in accord with the belief that *we are all one*, which is another way of saying that we're all connected. None of us can survive and evolve in total isolation. We're interdependent. As babies we require human touch and affection. Even in adulthood, we thrive in caring environments.

Another premise widely acknowledged in both the scientific and spiritual communities is that we all have a more or less latent anger—a *dark side*, if you will, especially if our means of survival are threatened.

Have you ever met a perfect person? Always right? Never made a mistake? While some may want to convey this impression, it's never completely true. None of us is alone in confronting our past mistakes or shortcomings. But dwelling incessantly in the past is not in our best interests and blaming others for everything that's gone wrong in our lives is self-destructive, since it's a form of denial that we were at least in large part responsible for our choices that led to our hardships. Denial or lack of acceptance of the duality of human nature often leads to a sense self-righteousness, which can result in conflicts within our minds and thus in our relationships with others that ultimately create confusion, sorrow and pain.

We can call anything negative that's ever happened a *learning experience*, which in fact it is, if we take the opportunity to actually learn from it. However, the term *learning experience* whitewashes all the negativity related to mistakes, faults, failures, and flaws—words that exist for specific reasons in describing human experience. For instance, when something negative happens that harms a relationship between two adults, usually both parties are responsible, at least to some extent, for the damage.

Finger pointing and scapegoating do nothing to solve any problem. While *failures* and *mistakes* are terms we try to avoid, we're not free to move on until we acknowledge them. It's more caring and responsible to accept that we're all connected—needing to rely on one another for acceptance, support and sustenance. The awakening of compassion is a natural result of recognizing our shared humanity, in all its facets.

The key action we must take in finding joy in our lives is to forgive others and ourselves for being a source of unhappiness. Forgiveness has never been based on worthiness. It's our acceptance of one another as flawed human beings and admission of our imperative to survive in a world where we're not devoured by hatred, especially self-hatred. It's only when we recognize our own role in creating conflict that we can see clearly that we're part of a larger picture in which we must live together. Our healthiest, happiest and most natural way of relating to each other is out of love.

Besides, *failure* is not a dirty word. Successful people are not afraid to fail. As a matter of fact, the most successful individuals fail time and time again, in unyielding efforts to succeed in realizing meaningful goals that are based on lifetime passions. Failure is a vital step on the path to ultimate victory. Experimentation is crucial in discovering anything worthwhile.

Once you become more self-aware you discover it's wise to accept your weaknesses as well as your strengths. Only then, you can accept the same in others, and feel compassion and forgiveness for others as well as yourself.

As you embark on your amazing journey from self-awareness toward becoming your best version of you and you recognize that you share some darker elements with all of humanity, you can make the conscious choice to extend forgiveness and compassion to your fellow men and women. At the same time, you can allow the self-love that you have been denying yourself to begin to heal and transform you as it brings new meaning into your life. Your renewed perspective of the vulnerability and accountability you share with humanity will actually build your inner strength and increase your openness to genuine love and joy.

THE MAGNETISM OF HIGHER CONSCIOUSNESS

Few of us are adept at expressing love for others, or in accepting their love toward us. But we can learn, and the joy is in the learning. Every form of love comes to us as a gift. That gift may be humble, or extended to us in an awkward way, but that doesn't diminish its value. If we accept the gift of love with grace and gratitude, we acknowledge its importance for the giver and for us. The art of giving and receiving love with gratitude enhances the meaning of life. Acceptance of love, and those with whom we share it, is more rewarding than criticizing others for their *lack* in satisfying our needs.

Happiness is an inside job. We're responsible for our own happiness. While others may try to make us happy with their love, they may find it a futile and thankless endeavor. And when we reject or begin to take for granted the gift of love from those who care about us, we may lose it.

There's a fine line between a passive form of *acceptance* and indifference or apathy. To actively accept acts of love and compassion from others—whatever the mode of expression—with our love, open-mindedness, and gratitude is the opposite of apathy. In fact, we move toward a *higher consciousness* when we expand our acceptance to include our sense of oneness with our latent family and friends and ultimately with the universe.

Research has suggested we are each sources of energy with a signature energy level determined by our frequency of vibrations. Our actions are a reflection of our beliefs. A growing body of evidence indicates *higher consciousness* or acceptance manifests higher vibrations than lower forms of awareness. Our level of acceptance includes our acceptance of self. So self-acceptance or confidence can at least in part determine our level of energy and in turn create a higher frequency of vibrations. Confidence is a key component of our credibility and in turn, determines our value to others.

A concept that's establishing scientific validity is *the law of attraction,* based on the premise that *like attracts like:* According to this theory, our universe is one big magnetic field in which *like* or similar energy vibrations are attracted to one another. From this we can reason that our energy waves attract similar waves from other people: as a result, our level of consciousness determines the level of consciousness—or energy—in those we attract. This means that as we grow and evolve, we're able to attract more like-minded people with minds open to new ideas, high ideals, and intangible concepts like love.

The Law of Attraction is a fascinating concept that's acquiring more legitimacy as we increase our understanding of the all-encompassing power of energy in our universe. It's certainly evident that when we project real confidence in ourselves, which—as opposed to arrogance—reflects a loving acceptance of others, we become more approachable, attractive, and lovable.

RAISING CONSCIOUSNESS
TO AN ART FORM

I n answering the question *Does art imitate life or does life imitate art?* I venture to say the relationship between art and human life is synergistic. In other words, art and life each nourish the other and at best transcend their literal union to embrace and convey a higher level of awareness, joy, and spirituality than either could attain without the other. But the best in humanity outdistances even the most *valuable* art.

For example, when an individual reads a good book, she or he is transported to another world that offers new awareness, enlightenment and inspiration. We might conclude the more highly rated the book, the more it touches the reader. If so, it follows that *great literature*—reading considered *art* by presumed experts—has superior power to move its readers to higher levels of consciousness. To a considerable extent, this is true. However, appreciating a book and reaching a more meaningful understanding of life from reading it are very subjective matters. People have widely varying tastes in regard to what constitutes good reading.

It's much the same with any other art form, including painting and all forms of visual art, music, and even film, which is a burgeoning form of artistic expression. While some works attract more attention than others, the most obscure painting, musical composition, or independent film may be extraordinary in its beauty to the eyes, ears, and emotions of its receptive audience, or even one person who finds transcendence to a higher state of awareness within a particular book, painting, sculpture, song, or film.

This power of art to uplift human consciousness also applies to its creators—probably even more than to those who read it, view it, hear it, or otherwise consume it. Artists, composers, writers, and film directors may spend months—quite possibly years—investing thoughts and feelings in their works of art. To refine and improve the quality of their self-expression, they often sacrifice what others would consider a normal life—including family life, material comforts, and leisure others might take for granted.

The question is: What is the source of inspiration for those who create art, music, books and film? While part of the source is likely other works of art, musical compositions, books, etc., which most creators study in relation to their craft, there needs to be something more—something that makes that individual's creation unique. It needs to be a statement that only he or she can share with the universe. It comes from deep within the creator's consciousness, emotions, senses—even his or her soul. It must have integrity; that is, it must be honest, according to that person's perceptions of reality and responses to life. All of this comes from his or her life experience, and conceivably the experience of his or her ancestors through genetic inheritance.

I believe the most powerful force on earth is love, expressed as a noun but also a verb. When we express love, offering it as a gift to others, we are acting on our highest level of consciousness. Our value as individual human beings is greater than any painting, book, song, or whatever art form we may create, especially when we consciously develop our capacity to give our love to those close to us and ideally to every human being. We can effectively develop our ability to love to the level of an art form though our daily communication. Sharing our love vastly increases our human potential. Ultimately, its influence expands and achieves immortality.

Our emotions, especially feelings of love, must be honest and authentic before they can hold any worthwhile meaning. Although it's often best to try to turn a negative situation into something more positive, our expression of love can't always be cheerful, happy-go-lucky, or jovial. Just like the best works of art express an array of complex emotions—a painting displays light tones against dark, a musical masterpiece blends major and minor keys—our strongest human feelings are so deep that they sometimes seem unfathomable. Emotions require our honest examination to express them with accuracy as they convey the love, compassion and honor that others deserve, by virtue of being human.

When our actions reflect our authentic self-expression—with love at the apex of our focus and hence our purpose—we are the creators of caring and meaningful lives. While art in all its beauty and wonder can enrich our lives, it's not a prerequisite to becoming fine human beings. Finally, a life well lived is never dependent on riches or fame to be a tour de force!

COMMUNICATION

COMMUNICATION MADE EASY

How much of what we say actually makes a desired impact on our target audience, whether it's one person, a group, or even a crowd?

People are always talking, but much of the interaction can be somewhat mindless. We're just filling the air with sound. When we improve our awareness of what we want to communicate to achieve a meaningful objective, we're on the right track, but we benefit even more when we learn the skills vital to our success in making a dynamic impact on our listeners.

First it's imperative we understand that each individual has a unique perspective on life, so while we may think we've said one thing, that person may have heard something entirely different. Our beliefs often influence how we receive another person's words. Expressing religious or political ideas to an audience of one or more with different beliefs may elicit a strong reaction, but not necessarily the one the speaker wants, unless she or he is trying to stir controversy.

Topics that seem rather innocuous by comparison can also raise strong objections. If listeners voice their protests to a certain concept, an argument can result. This doesn't mean that we should avoid any form of conflict. Conflict is an essential part of life and—like variety—it gives life its spice!

There are ways to engage in conflict without raising anger. Knowing how to listen is just as important to successful communication as knowing how to speak. The one common factor is keeping an open mind. Just because someone doesn't think exactly as we do doesn't make her or him wrong.

When we keep our presentation friendly and open to discussion we're allowing opportunities for varying points of view without creating an atmosphere of hostility. Diplomacy is a valuable skill. Some simple tips can help to maintain cooperation and calm in the potential heat of battle. Keep in mind *easy does it!*

As a speaker:

- Smile.
- Take time to breathe.
- Use gentle humor, not sarcasm.
- Make open gestures or keep your arms at your sides.
- Maintain a calm and warm tone of voice.
- Ask open-ended but non-invasive questions.
- Maintain an erect but relaxed body posture.
- Nod to let whoever is responding know you're listening.
- Repeat someone's statement, to clarify her or his meaning.
- Avoid words or gestures that indicate blame, judgment, or ridicule.
- Research the topic beforehand, if possible.
- Stay focused on the issues—don't get personal.

It's wise to remember that there's often a blurred line between difference of opinion and *bias,* which can be defined as *prejudice in favor of or against one thing, person, or group compared with another, usually in a way considered to be unfair.* A bias is frequently based on a stereotype, which is the assumption that all members of a group—such as women—have the same traits; for instance, "All women are too emotional." This is clearly an unfair bias. Beyond this, it's irrational. First of all, exactly what does "too emotional" mean? When someone expresses this kind of bias, it's probably best to avoid getting into a heated debate, unless you're sure you have the perfect finesse to avoid disaster. Besides if you impulsively react to this comment, which might be said to goad you, you could be *proving* that your opponent is correct in his or her biased assertion.

HOW DO YOU MAKE
OTHERS FEEL?

T he most basic principle I have to share with you about conversation is how you make people feel is what they will remember long after your words fade away in their memory. This may be the most important axiom you can learn in conversing with effectiveness. Honestly, if you just keep this in mind whenever you engage in conversation, you will be way ahead of the game.

It's so simple, but sometimes we forget, don't care, or simply don't understand how our words fail to have the impact we desire: It's largely our attitude when we speak that makes a positive or negative impression, often even more than the words we're saying. Attitude is everything, and I'm suggesting you convey an open accepting attitude of kindness and fairness, not a bossy or condescending approach to talking with others.

A conversation is communication that takes place between two or more individuals. Within this context, there's a very specific etiquette: one person talks while the other(s) listen. Effectual listening is just as important as interesting or persuasive speech.

But imagine a listener's dismay when he or she is patiently trying to take in all that the speaker is saying, while the speaker seems to have little or no intention of giving that listener a chance to respond or ask questions. My guess is that it won't require much imagination for you to recognize this scenario: it happens all too often. When it does, even if the listener doesn't overtly object, the speaker has probably lost his or her interest and respect.

The hard truth is that whenever one of us has the opportunity to express our concepts, opinions, or points of view, we quickly lose our audience if we become absorbed in ourselves, to the exclusion of anyone who happens to hear us speak. When we become self-aggrandizing, self-righteous or self-centered in any way, when we presume to give advice with the certainty that our wisdom outdistances that of the person or people we're advising, or when we assume we have the last word on any topic, our audience is lost and may be hurt or offended. At the very least those listening find us to be a bore and probably a bully, since we've abused valuable time, dominated the conversation, and shown total disregard for possible injured feelings.

Frankly, I find it difficult to believe any speaker can be ignorant in all these respects. And yet I've witnessed it time and again. The speaker will interpret any listener's good manners as license to *filibuster* what might have been a perfectly good exchange between or among equal participants.

A conversation is not by definition a competition, but I've seen both men and women talking at one another as though rivalry is the prescribed intent. A conversation could better be described as a *negotiation*, at best a pleasant one, in which the shared outcome is win-win, not win-lose!

THE ART OF PERSUASION

Communication at its best is not just the exchange of information. It's the mastery of getting information *through* to your audience. To accomplish this, it's essential that you first attract its attention. And then you must convince that audience that what you have to say is worth maintaining an interest or better yet heightening awareness in what is being said.

To communicate with effectiveness it's necessary that you develop some skills in the art of persuasion. Unlike manipulation, which is coercing people to do things your way even though it may not be in their best interest, persuasion is the art of influencing others to do things that are in their best interests and perhaps ours, as well.

Successful people in business—especially in advertising, marketing, and sales—understand that in order to sell a product or service, they must communicate its *benefits*, which can be thought of as solutions to human problems or needs—often psychological. For example, toothpaste is not sold simply on the basis of its features—like white, comes in a tube—but rather the benefits the user enjoys, such as a brighter smile and confidence in attracting potential admirers, when using a particular brand.

Another basic principle of persuasion is that while human beings have the potential to share high ideals, including the desire to help others, our basic needs for food, water, and shelter must be satisfied before we're free to implement serving our more selfless objectives.

Whenever you communicate to persuade others that something will be to their advantage, you must appeal to their specific and dominant needs. Achieving this requires research: it's vital to ask your potential audience questions to ascertain their greatest needs. Then you can determine how your product or service offers a solution in meeting those needs.

If you're starting from scratch, without a product or service in mind, create one that will benefit your audience in terms of serving your clients' or customers' psychological and physiological needs as well. The more exacting, in-depth, and detailed a description you use to address those needs, the more likely you'll succeed in resonating with them—convincing them that you have an effective solution to their problem(s).

In addition to presenting your message in a context that's relevant to your specific audience, persuasion becomes more influential when you 1) personalize your message so your audience can easily relate to it; 2) use a story to illustrate your message; 3) use a demo; and 4) present some fascinating evidence.

If you combine these strategies with positive, compassionate energy in delivering your message, you'll not only be a master persuader, you'll be providing your audience—whether on person or millions comprise it— with something that offers a genuine answer to its deepest needs and desires.

The Universal Power
of a Smile

Sometimes the simplest concepts are also the most profound. Our attitudes are vitally important in communicating with others. The attitude we convey supersedes our words, whether we're in conversation or speaking to a group. Even without words, our attitudes surpass all other factors in influencing our interactions with family, friends, co-workers, and strangers.

We can't control others' behavior. We can only control our reaction to it—or much better, our mindful response. But let's face it: To our own vexation, most of us don't have total control of our attitude all the time. In fact, our emotional responses can include sadness, anger, and frustration—just to name a few—within a single day or even an hour. While we try our best to keep a positive attitude, we're multifaceted human beings, not automatons, and sometimes, maybe often, our negative feelings surface from that private place inside to the brave exterior we present to the world.

While it can be difficult to stop our feelings from flaring at inopportune times, there are a few ways we can respect our emotions, without allowing them to poison our relationships. No doubt the best remedy for a *bad mood* is to smile. I know, it seems so easy, yet how many of us practice it? You'll be amazed at the results if you cultivate the habit of smiling at other people in public places, even when you're sad or hurt or don't especially feel like smiling for one reason or another. Much of the time, a smile generates an immediate smile from the party you're smiling at. Not only does this give you the opportunity to brighten another's day, but it also brightens yours. I urge you to try it if you don't do this already.

Smiling really is a universal language, and it usually works—sometimes in unexpected but very pleasant ways. For one thing, sadness, stress, and other negative feelings can drain us of energy, making us feel tired and fatigued. But a smile has power to energize us, even as it elevates our mood. Every time you smile and someone smiles back at you, you're likely to feel a little better—even happy—and you'll have more positive energy to do whatever it you're intending to do that day.

Sometimes the other person doesn't smile back. Don't let this bother you. If your smile worked 100% of the time, it would have little meaning. If you decide to experiment with the habit of smiling, you'll get the most interesting results if you smile at those you don't expect to smile back, as well as the easy *targets*, who already look cheerful. If you don't discriminate, you have more of a challenge and more potential for good. Besides, you never know where a smile might lead.

Don't feel obliged to constantly share a toothy grin with the universe. You can think kinds thoughts, smile with your lips closed, and let your smiling eyes do the talking. You can develop your own signature smile, but it's best if it comes from your heart. I don't advise that you just walk around with a smile plastered on your face. I think it's more natural, and real, if the other party sees you break out into a gentle smile at seeing them. Then there's a chance for a communion of kindred spirits, if only for a moment, but the good feeling that results can last for a lovely interlude, perhaps all day or at least until the next smile.

You may notice that you're almost always the first one to smile whenever you approach or even glance at someone. You're entitled to feel good that you're the first to dare to reach out. Besides, you'll become more aware about one aspect of human nature: Many people—if not most—will wait for another person to show some sign of friendliness, before they choose to respond or ignore their overture of kindness. It's as though they believe that their egos will be irreversibly damaged if their smiles don't evoke a positive response. This actually isn't likely. Friendliness is usually contagious. And a few rejections are more than worth the rewards.

In any event, when you replace the fear of rejection with the love and courage to smile, you'll discover that it sometimes leads to an enjoyable exchange of words or even a new friendship. Smiling won't break your face, or your heart, and every smile holds the potential for new beginnings!

REPLACING IDLE COMPLAINTS WITH VIABLE SOLUTIONS

While we're all compelled to vent on occasion, most of us would be wise to take stock in just how much we complain. Too much and it's whining, especially when we don't have solutions to our problems.

There are times when a session of protesting all of life's injustices with a close friend can be absolutely cathartic, especially when our friend empathizes with us, assuring us that our feelings of anger are *spot on*. Still, the number of times we indulge in this ritual should remain few and far between and limited to our most intimate companions, whom we trust as completely as possible. Otherwise, we're better off keeping our lips sealed.

While complaining may offer you some temporary relief from your fury, it doesn't really solve anything. And while your friends may have your best interests at heart, they don't walk in your shoes, so if you go to them for counsel, be prepared for unwanted advice that you may end up resenting. Remember, once you share your problem, you can't take it back. If you value your relationship, you don't want to jeopardize it just to get someone else's input and satisfy your more-or-less idle curiosity.

A problem with your marriage or your children is very personal. To disclose it to anyone else can be a significant betrayal of your family member's trust. Besides, you may be implicitly asking your friend to take sides, and that can backfire on everyone involved, especially when you get past your anger and you're ready to forgive the subject of your complaints.

Confronting a loved one with a complaint—especially over and over—is *nagging*, which can be extremely damaging to any relationship. A much better choice is to talk with your family member or friend in a non-blaming way about your feelings in response to his or her behavior. Together you can negotiate a solution to your problem that ideally satisfies you both.

The act of complaining also has a way of transitioning into gossip about a third party who may have offended you—perhaps without even meaning to do any harm. It's patently unfair to talk about someone behind his or her back. Others have a right to form their own opinions regarding an individual, and the person in question has a right to make his or impression on others without your influence. Besides your gossip signals friends that you may complain about them as well, which undermines their trust in you.

Some people have developed a habit or complaining. If you have a teensy-weensy tendency to complain, perhaps it's time to remind yourself to stop. Note the times you complain throughout a day or a week. Rather than punish yourself when you complain, reward yourself when you don't. This may give you the motivation to quit, once and for all.

I know the best version of you is above pettiness. You're a much bigger person than any weak actions may indicate. Aspire to bring out that great person inside you who thrives on self-expression and genuine loving relationships. It feels so much better to be accepting and compassionate than to experience remorse when you complain with harshness to a loved one or say something hurtful about someone you know.

If you're hard-pressed for something new to talk about, develop a fresh curiosity about the world around you. There are fascinating things to learn everywhere we look. Follow current events or a particular topic that interests you. What excites you? What moves you? What mystery would you like to unfold? What do you like to read? Where would you l like to travel? How would you most like to spend your time? What could you do to make the world a better place? Incorporate the topics that most interest you into your conversations. You'll find avenues of enjoyment that you had overlooked.

Idle complaining is always futile; on the other hand, taking the time to come up with a solution to a problem is always time well spent. It just takes a simple but enormous shift in attitude that everyone will notice, including you. Instead of being the one to focus on problems, be the woman who comes up with creative and caring solutions to the issues that concern you. You'll feel the empowering freedom of increased self-esteem. And the universe will thank you.

THE IMPOSSIBILITY OF
TELLING IT LIKE IT IS

I don't want to micro-manage anyone's most intimate conversations: as unique individuals, we each have every right to choose our words and how we say them. But I want to encourage all women to realize the power of our words and behavior, which ultimately impacts us—sometimes in profound ways that we don't consciously acknowledge.

Our freedom, our power, and our right to communicate our thoughts as authentic women comprises inherent responsibility— even at micro-levels. When we stop to think about our smallest and most seemingly insignificant verbal or nonverbal exchanges with other human beings, we can begin to see patterns that may not be working for anyone's benefit, including our own.

First, being authentic isn't about *telling it like it* is, because there is no such thing. There is no ultimate truth, no objective right or wrong, no measure of good or bad, but only what we perceive as being so. We cross a line of propriety when we become blaming or judgmental, based on our limited concept of *how it is.*

When we're speaking with someone, the only way we can keep our perception of reality within the bounds of fairness, it to address how something makes us feel—whether or not it's based on another person's words or actions. We always have a right to our feelings, but the rule of civility in any fair exchange is to keep the lines of communication open so that we can resolve any potential problem.

In your personal and public life, if something someone has said or done has hurt you, the best way to maintain open communication is to state how you feel in a non-blaming way. But first it's wise to decide how important it is to let that person know about your bruised feelings. This depends on your real motivation: Are you telling that individual about your feelings to improve the relationship or do you just want to *get even* by hurting the person in question with your objections? If you're not trying to reach a mutual understanding, the hurtful words or actions are likely to continue—even escalate—until perhaps the relationship fails altogether.

On the other hand, if you're honestly trying to reach an agreement, solve a problem, and keep positive lines of communication open, yet still the other party continues with the wounding behavior, perhaps that relationship isn't worth the time you invest, not to mention your resulting stress. It's always your choice to maintain any connection or move on. If it's an abusive relationship within your home, I suggest you seek professional help and if that doesn't work, call a safe and reputable hotline to find out what to do with minimum threat to your safety.

Scolding, finger pointing, accusing, or blaming are largely ineffective ways to stimulate positive change. It's often most damaging among family members. It's more advantageous to set aside a time to discuss an issue calmly and without finding fault to resolve things in a way that allows mutual satisfaction. In other words, always think win-win!

In casual conversations with friends or acquaintances, it can be easy to get annoyed or offended by something another has said, even though that person may not have tried to hurt your feelings. Sometimes it really can be best to give the other party the benefit of the doubt, and assume their negative comment was inadvertent. But if happens repeatedly, it may be time to call it into question. Still, we lose control when we lose our temper, so it's probably wise to give ourselves a cooling off period before we confront that person about the matter that's bothering us.

The power of words is often much stronger than we acknowledge, and we share the same moral obligation as everyone else to avoid being insensitive with our use of language. Before you decide to criticize anyone, ask yourself if it's difficult to tell that person what he or she needs to hear, or whether it's giving you some pleasure to put that individual in his or her *place*. If it's the latter, it's probably smart to refrain. Otherwise, you're just going to make the world a little bit meaner.

When you apply kindness in overcoming your ego, you release its trap of attaching too much importance to your own thoughts and emotions, which separate you from others—and you allow love to triumph.

WALKING YOUR TALK
BODY LANGUAGE

One of my primary goals in writing *Women Who Walk the Talk* is to inspire you to say exactly what you mean with confidence and effectiveness, no matter what influences seem undermine you. These influences can be outside forces—such as pressure from family and friends—or they can be internal, based on your own limiting beliefs about your value and potential. In order to say what you mean, it's vital that you appreciate your unique value and think for yourself.

Your best approach in any situation is to walk your talk, saying your truth in your own unique voice, and allowing your body language to reinforce your words. Otherwise, no matter how lofty your speech, you may be judged as an imposter.

Speaking woman to woman, I know that using complete honesty in expressing how you feel isn't always an easy matter. Many of us have developed a noble but self-sabotaging habit of putting others first—the men in our lives, our children, and our employers—and trying to project that we're totally fine, while we bury our frustration and try to hide our breaking spirits. While we're adept at multi-tasking and overextending ourselves, our efforts to seem composed aren't really working at an optimal level.

You may be surprised to learn that actual speech comprises less than 10% of our communication with others, body language over 50%, and tone of voice the remaining 40%. While a greater awareness of our nonverbal communication can help us to convey more confidence and make a more positive impression, most experts agree that it's impossible to completely control how others interpret what we're saying with our body language.

Since most of our body language is determined at a subconscious level, its manifestation is subtle and complex, so while we may think we're successful at convincing others of an untruth—or effectively telling a lie—they're likely to read our nonverbal cues and detect our efforts at deception. Women are often found to be particularly receptive to nonverbal cues.

Studies have shown that someone will make an assessment about a person within the first seconds of meeting—and decide whether he or she will like that individual. Clearly, this doesn't give any of us much time to *put up a good front*. While most people can read others' body language with remarkable acuity without formal training, some signals to recognize when someone is being untruthful are:

- Glancing away/sideways glancing
- Forced eye contact
- Stiff posture
- Fidgeting
- Hand hiding
- Pupil contraction
- Controlled vocal tone
- Stutters, slurs, and hesitations
- Sweating
- Giggling

Another interesting clue that betrays your frame of mind is pointing your feet in a direction that reveals you're ready to leave, rather than toward the person with whom you're sharing a conversation.

Some of these behaviors could indicate self-consciousness or shyness. The best remedy for any sort of uneasiness it to focus on the other person, and concentrate on making that individual comfortable, rather than riveting on the impression you're making. Besides, it's wise to question the source of your nervousness. Are you trying to hide something you'd be embarrassed to reveal? If you're selling a product or service, is it something you believe in?

Avoiding potentially awkward situations by keeping it all inside is not a proactive resolution to a problem. Perhaps someone seems to be taking you for granted, or isn't doing his or her share of the housework: instead of secretly fuming about it and expecting the other party to read your mind, plan ahead how to arrange a peaceful conversation and reach a solution that both parties accept.

The adage that no one's going to believe in you until you believe in yourself is true. But a sense of self-worth can't be accomplished overnight. Take it easy on yourself: set aside time to engage in activities you enjoy in order to become a happier individual. Set specific goals to develop your authenticity. When you learn to relax and be yourself, self-assurance will replace self-consciousness, and you'll be astonished how much easier it is to elicit a more favorable response from others.

Still, it's no light matter. Your integrity and your credibility are defined by your actions and the nonverbal cues you project as well as your speech. Even more important, your health and wellbeing determine your state of mind. Take the time to practice self-care and self-love. And then let the best you—and that's always the real you—shine through. Make it a firm practice to walk your talk.

OPEN COMMUNICATION
NOURISHES RELATIONSHIPS

Relationships—especially loving ones—are meant to go forward in achieving shared goals, enhancing mutual values, establishing parameters, and discovering new paths to increased intimacy. A relationship can stand still and meet minimum standards for comfort and convenience. Or both partners may give one another plenty of space to pursue their separate objectives. These are viable choices that are not uncommon.

But most of us would probably agree that the ideal relationship is one in which each person has at least some of his or her emotional needs met by a caring partner. For this, it's imperative we get beyond the *small talk*. A relationship is a connection and exchange between two people. This means confronting the tough issues, so a healthy intimacy can grow.

Ideally, people in committed relationships make time to talk without distractions on a somewhat regular basis in order to discuss potential difficulties at an early stage. Any relationship can improve if each person pays earnest attention to the other individual and honestly examines his or her own actions before finding fault with the other. Especially in a romantic relationship, each needs to be non-judgmental in listening to his or her mate, and show genuine interest in what the he or she is experiencing. Then both parties will be working as a team in making the best of the relationship. In a fair argument there are no winners or losers: the goal is mutual accord.

In any relationship, listen carefully to what your friend, loved one, or business associate is trying to say. Never dismiss his or her thoughts. Keep the discussion positive and don't let it get heated; if it does, take a time out. Be truthful and direct about your own feelings, but express them in a caring manner and use body language that matches your words. In other words, walk you talk.

While these ideas seem reasonable, common sense is not always easy to apply when dealing with the human heart, which is unfathomable. Long- term relationships, and in particular romantic ones based on trust and intimacy must be nurtured to survive, because they involve two vulnerable human beings. Relationships are as fragile as the feelings invested. Trust doesn't always come easily, nor do I think it should. Love is a learning process—one of give and take.

That said, loving relationships should be fun and, in fact, they usually are. Maybe the suggestions herein sound like a lot of work. But I can guarantee you that living by these principles is a lot less work than trying to maintain control over another by insisting you're always right. At the same time, it's humiliating to remain in someone else's control. For the most part, control is just an illusion, created with bullying tactics and deception. The resulting imbalance is damaging; it ultimately destroys most relationships.

Any relationship is more dynamic when it's based on mutual respect for the real feelings of both individuals. Manipulation is useless compared to the honesty and openness required to achieve a caring union of equals.

How to Ask for Help

Many of us don't ask for help out of fear that it's admitting to weakness. On the contrary, when we demonstrate humility we can sometimes earn the respect of others. In business, asking for help can even be viewed as a sign of integrity, especially if the request is coupled with a willingness to act in collaboration with others.

Our fears in asking for help can be overcome with a little effort. While we may be concerned that our request is placing a burden on others, at the same time we miss an opportunity to show them how we value and respect them. Usually, a person is more than glad to help another achieve a worthwhile goal—especially if it's a shared one. We should be cautious from whom we ask for help; however, or we could find ourselves at the wrong end of a patronizing, controlling and unbalanced relationship.

Timing is crucial. Asking for help as soon as you realize you need it can avoid your frustration, angst, and perhaps a risk of failure. For example, you may want to ask a co-worker for his or her expertise before you complete a project at work, in order to meet a deadline. If you're asking for outside assistance from your boss, focus on the benefit for the company. Even if you're worried about a possible negative outcome, don't whine or express panic. Your request doesn't necessarily indicate a lack of competence on your part. In fact, asking for help doesn't by definition diminish your strengths at all. Some tips to remember when asking for help are as follows:

- Evaluate what it will take to achieve a successful outcome.
- Ask early for a time that's convenient to the other person to talk.
- State up front what it is you need and be direct.
- Be clear and specific in your request.
- Have a clear objective. Make it positive and interesting.
- Have options in mind. One is, "Can you suggest something else?"
- Be ready to explore alternatives.
- Use the help that's offered.

After someone has helped you, it's important that you express your gratitude and show a genuine desire to reciprocate. Most people prefer a give-and-take relationship, because the balance of power shifts when we're dependent on another, and we don't like to feel indebted.

Successful people understand their own areas of proficiency. And they know how to surround themselves with others who are good at everything else. Remember, we have nothing to lose if we ask for help in the right context. The real risk is in trying to do everything alone.

SELF-ACTUALIZATION
AND ITS HAZARDS

THE INEFFECTIVENESS OF PLAYING DUMB

To play dumb is to pretend to be slow-witted or lacking in specific knowledge, usually in order to avoid responsibility or gain some advantage. While anyone can play dumb in any number of circumstances, it's a tactic that's often been ascribed to women, especially in regard to our relationships with men. To be fair, the reason some women exhibit this behavior has also been explained as an effort to bolster men's egos. Whatever the reason, it's not smart.

Women have traditionally been known to sacrifice our self-respect, as well as our potential, for the sake of a relationship. While this practice is less prevalent today than it has been in recent history, it still exists, as well as the negative consequences. This can apply to relationships between a man and a woman as well as two women.

If someone we've been deceiving with our *mental inferiority* becomes a marital partner, this could mean keeping up the hoax for a lifetime—a sad waste of intellect, not to mention energy—resources we could better spend developing a relationship based on mutual respect, a process that's more enjoyable and more empowering to each party involved..

In regard to a relationship with a man in particular, no matter the reason a woman hides her intelligence, it's not good enough. If a man is so insecure that he needs a *stupid* woman to make him look good, he's not worth the effort it takes to provide him with the illusion that he's the smarter partner. Besides, when he decides he's superior—maybe even too good for her—she's created a monster, and the relationship is doomed.

But to a confident male, an intelligent woman is actually more attractive. She's not dependent or needy, and she can uphold her end of a conversation. She communicates more confidence, too—a very engaging trait. We can imagine two women in the same scenario.

Clearly when you're unattached you have plenty of time to discover a potential partner, based on qualities besides physical attraction that reveal his or her character and capacity for love and commitment. It's best to be realistic rather than overly modest about your assets, and it's crucial to establish your values in selecting a future mate who will in fact be your equal. Plus it's fair for you to expect that the man or woman in question is one who will allow you to grow and self-actualize.

To learn whether a potential love interest shares similar standards, you can simply ask questions—not in an *in your face* sort of way, but with friendliness, even playfulness, so no one is embarrassed, including you. On the other hand, if you're in a rush toward commitment, maybe it's time to ease up and slow down. Authentic happiness is worth the time it takes to achieve it.

Emotional intelligence—at least as valuable to an individual as bookish smarts—is an attribute distinguished by social responsibility, interpersonal skills, tolerance to stress and impulse control. A lack of assertiveness in applying these aptitudes can be viewed as a weakness. It's crucial to balance assertiveness and boundaries with your other emotional strengths in order to advocate yourself and develop your self-esteem.

Let your intelligence shine. If you want to become brainier, read more, take classes and discuss various topics of mutual interest with friends. Become an expert in an area that fascinates you. Go for the career you've always dreamed of. Stay independent until you're ready for commitment. By the way, there's no law that says you're ever required to marry. Just keep your mind active and don't hide that beautiful brain of yours under a rock.

Skilled negotiators are never perceived as needy. If you think negotiation is reserved for high-powered careers, it's time to think again. Marriage is a lifetime of negotiation, at least when it's done right. All successful relationships are based on negotiation, cooperation, and a little compromise, so that both parties triumph.

One caveat: no one likes a know-it-all. But there's a huge difference between 1) being aggressive in your arrogance and, 2) knowing how to communicate your intelligence with subtlety, kindness, and charm.

WHEN WOMEN HONOR WOMEN WE ALL WIN

Throughout history, men have upheld a system of hierarchy: they compete to attain power. Those who win become leaders. Although this dominant cultural norm has created its own set of evils, it's also preserved a flawed but accepted order that more-or-less works in getting things done.

As differentiated from men, throughout most of history women have established a more egalitarian culture, founded on a standard of nurturing, which requires cooperation. While this is noble, there's a downside that prevails when the concept of standards declines to insistence on uniformity.

As more women enter the work force, a family with a stay-at-home mom is no longer the *norm*. In fact, limitless options—ranging from motherhood to career—are open to women today. Because we're the queens of empathy, we understand that all life choices are valid. Or do we? Perhaps our understanding of women's rights to make choices hasn't caught up to the diverse choices we're making in adapting to the demands of modern culture.

Equally probable, those of us who are working outside the home may not be comfortable in our new capacity as competitors for power and income and we're still feeling awkward in filling the role. As we grow in awareness and experience the frustration and exhaustion of working to *make it* alone, we realize a greater demonstration of empathy and respect among women would be a welcome factor in promoting our shared advancement—regardless of what choices we make as individuals

Competition in itself isn't a dirty word. It doesn't require cutthroat tactics like backstabbing. The most effective leaders understand this. Respecting our rivals —whether male or female—and treating them with fairness, despite our vying objectives, is the world-class way to travel on our journey to success, since everybody has a chance to win or lose with dignity. Besides each *loss* or *failure* is just a learning experience on the way to ultimate success—a personal matter for each individual throughout life.

In truth, we can expedite women's progress at a faster rate when we realize one basic fact: Our vital obligation to support one another goes beyond mere acceptance. It's tantamount to respecting—even celebrating—one another's differences, not just within our families and circle of friends, but in our community, and on a global level. But how do we demonstrate our active support of other women?

It starts on a personal level. Perhaps the most essential way we can show our respect toward another woman is to listen when she speaks, without interruption. Then, in responding —not reacting— to her, we refrain from criticism or condescending advice. If she asks our opinion we can offer our point of view. But we must avoid invalidating her, or minimizing her feelings, by saying things like, "You don't understand." We can withhold judgment and make acceptance of another women's life decisions a priority, since we each have a right to human dignity equal to anyone on the planet.

We can cultivate the art of conversation with other women when we encourage them to feel free to talk openly within congenial surroundings. To accomplish this, we can develop the habit of asking questions, which allow our feminine friends to talk about their needs, values, passions, goals, dreams, and ideas without fear of being rejected, denounced, or ridiculed; and we can make a diligent effort to offer genuine empathy and open-minded acceptance in response to their self-disclosure. Anything we say which suggests our superiority or overrides their concerns violates the ground rules of rapport between or among equals.

Of course, our words mean little if we don't back them up with actions. For example, in business, we can mentor, counsel, partner or consult with other women—helping them realize their full potentials in their careers. In every aspect of life, we are at our most humane when we offer our time, our emotional support and our resources without strings attached.

On the other hand, when we become controlling with our feminine peers, our intentions aren't always innocent. Instead they may be based on our proclivity to *compare and contrast,* the result of 1) our conditioning to enforce equalization among our species or 2) an ego-based compulsion to compete.

When one of our female colleagues dares to be different—rather than mirror our image—we may react with alarm, since we don't understand or appreciate her actions. We may even voice our objections to her independent stance—often based on our own feelings of inadequacy or fear of exclusion. We might even demand that she hang on tight to the *sameness loop*, where group approval is mandatory.

The enforcement of sameness often reveals the *enforcer* as smug, complacent, and bigoted, rather than someone who's enlightened concerning all women's rights to liberty and honor. It can be based on ignorance, unfair moral judgment, or envy. As women, all of our decisions are based on one basic choice: whether we want to support or inhibit our advancement as well as other women's progress toward becoming our true selves. This choice is ours alone, and doesn't require another's permission, just as other women don't require our approval to pursue life on their terms.

We can empower one another when we demonstrate our respect for each other's choices. When we honor our diversity, we free ourselves as well as others to reach our highest potential as authentic individuals—each with a unique gift to contribute. This in turn awakens the potential for shared accomplishment and invaluable synergy among collaborating team members, which empowers us all in our diverse but united objectives, as our solidarity provides more opportunity for achievement and power than one woman could accomplish alone.

HOW TO RECOGNIZE CONTROLLING PEOPLE

C ontrolling people can be difficult, to say the least. While at times they don't realize they're driving others away with their manipulative tactics, their actions are often deliberate in their efforts to sabotage our endeavors to grow and self-actualize. Once we recognize their specific traits, we can develop a strategy to respond to them with effectiveness and free ourselves from their controlling and often scheming ways.

Below are several characteristics that describe controlling people. If someone in your life exhibits any of the following behaviors, he or she could be attempting to control you.

Controlling people...

- expect you to alter your views, plans, or personality to fit theirs.
- are unhappy and try to improve their situation by controlling others.
- try to cause problems between you and your family or friends.
- are stingy with compliments.
- have temper outbursts.
- blame you for everything—nothing is ever their fault.
- simulate their physical pain if they think they're losing control.
- criticize or demean others as a way of building themselves up.
- must always "win" and get their own way.

- give orders and make demands, expecting to be the boss and be obeyed.
- give false information and present a false self.
- frustrate the efforts of others and undermine their plans.
- hurt others to prove they have the power to do so.
- use tactics of aggression and intimidation.

If someone is continually putting you in a subservient position—leveraging himself or herself to a pedestal from which he or she can look down upon you—that person is manipulative and controlling. These individuals frequently display narcissistic traits, including a need for admiration and a lack of empathy.

When a person is opinionated, it doesn't mean he or she is controlling, as long as he or she is willing to accept your differences. So try to be judicious in reaching a fair assessment. But just as important, be fair with yourself. If that individual is making you feel miserable because you never seem to meet his or her expectations except to satisfy an insatiable desire to *best* you, he or she is a controlling person using unfair tactics to manipulate you. If his or her behavior gets to the point that it's causing you undue stress—and perhaps you no longer like or respect this person—it's time to do something about it. In fact, it could be time to stop talking and start walking.

HOW TO RESPOND TO
CONTROLLING PEOPLE

I t can be extremely frustrating to try to deal with a controlling person. Unless we have specific tools, it might even be an exercise in futility. This is because there is no reasoning with him or her. But once we apply new awareness of how to respond to someone who's controlling, we can free ourselves from his or her manipulative behavior.

As soon as you realize another person in your life—perhaps your mate or a friend—is trying to control you, it becomes imperative to release yourself from that control and try to restore balance to the relationship. If this proves to be impossible, it may be time to distance yourself at least emotionally from this individual, who has a toxic effect on you.

When you're trying to liberate yourself from someone else's control, one thing to remember is that your objective is to change your behavior, not his or hers. During disagreements, individuals vary in their willingness to engage in conflict. Often, more passive people or those known as *people pleasers* will immediately give up or give in to restore peace. If the other party in the relationship is a controller, always needing to win, there's little chance for a balanced relationship. In fact, the stress that results from allowing yourself to be controlled can actually interfere with your immune system. In other words, it can literally make you ill. If you're permitting someone to control you, you're contributing to this pattern. Keeping your good health should always be your priority. In an effort to keep your wellbeing and safety intact, try to always remain calm. Learn to respond, not react, to his or her constant criticisms and demands.

When entering into dialogue with a controller, show that person the same respect that you desire. Emphasize positive things. Ask questions in an attempt to understand this person. In a conflicted conversation, stay focused on the topic at hand, rather than getting personal. Ideally, your goal is mutual cooperation. In reality, this may not be the controller's objective.

If your positivity isn't resulting in a collaborative outcome, you can point out to the controlling person that his or her behavior is making you uncomfortable, but be assertive so their problems don't become yours. While it's best to stand firm on the fact that you won't accept his or her control, remain composed. Keep in mind it's within your power to set boundaries in your relationship. Allowing someone to talk down to you is demeaning. Don't let it happen.

If you disagree with someone's inaccurate or inappropriate criticism, simply say, "I don't agree." Any brief and rational explanation is much more convincing than a lengthy defense. If a controller tells you you're doing something all wrong, you can politely disagree, but be aware that he or she will likely conclude you're mistaken.

Controlling people are constantly compelled to feel the power of influencing other people and they must see evidence of that influence. While we all have self-centered tendencies, and try to control our environment to some degree to suit our purposes, the most controlling people are regarded as *narcissists*. In its extreme form, *narcissistic syndrome* is considered a mental disorder, which occurs when an individual is completely self-serving, with no regard for the rights or feelings of others. If your partner's efforts to control you seem to be crossing the line into the realm of verbal abuse, you should seek counseling right away, before the problem escalates.

Not to be an alarmist, but verbal abuse can be as harmful as physical abuse. Beyond this, it sometimes advances into forms of domestic violence—endangering you and any children you may have. If counseling doesn't work, it may be necessary to leave an abusive situation, so research your options ahead of time in private and always keep your own and your children's safety a top priority. Don't hesitate to report physical abuse to authorities. The Domestic Violence Hotline, which offers 24/7 service in all 50 states, is 1-800-799-SAFE, (7233). If you believe you're in immediate danger, it can be vital to call 911.

THE DAMAGING EFFECTS
OF INVALIDATION

The practice of invalidating one another in everyday conversation is so prevalent that many of us probably don't even recognize when we're engaging in this behavior. We may even think we're helping another to cope with something that's causing emotional stress when we say "don't worry" or "you're taking things too seriously." But if we invalidate men, women, or children, even unwittingly, it's quite possible that we learned this way of relating to others from family members, authority figures and peers when we ourselves were children and adolescents. I had an *aha* moment when I first discovered that invalidation is an attempt to control another's feelings. One can reject, ignore, judge, mock, tease, refute, or diminish how someone feels: It's all considered invalidation.

Invalidation occurs when someone orders you to feel or look differently, as when he or she says, "Get over it" "Don't look so sad" or "Don't' get angry." Someone could deny your perception by saying something like "You've got it all wrong." He or she might tell you how you should feel or act with a comment such as "You should feel ashamed of yourself" and may even use reason, saying "You're not being rational" and debate with you in doing so. One might influence you to question yourself, asking "What's wrong with you?" Further, a person could judge or label you with a remark like "You're impossible" or "You're over-reacting." There are dozens of other examples of invalidation. It's a form of *emotional dishonesty* that goes beyond mere criticism in asserting or implying that someone is somehow abnormal, when this isn't the reality.

When invalidation is practiced repeatedly within a relationship, it's considered a form of verbal abuse. Consideration for our emotions is important to our mental and physical health. We need to feel respected and acknowledged. Invalidation is a form of emotional betrayal.

Invalidation is especially harmful to a child who learns to believe his or her emotions aren't real or worth consideration. When this happens, he or she begins to associate the expression of feelings with pain. This can be extremely damaging, because that young person is likely to grow into an adult who's in denial of his or her feelings. The experience of recurring invalidation from others during childhood is enough to damage anyone's sense of selfhood, confidence, and creativity in her or his self-expression.

It's not uncommon for a couple to develop a consistent habit of invalidating one another, which is unhealthy and sometimes mutually abusive behavior. If a disagreement develops between two people, a good principle is to first accept the other person's feelings as valid and important.

Awareness of invalidation and the harm it can do can help us curtail its destructive effects. If you begin to tell someone to "Don't be upset" first consider that if someone said this to you, it could make you feel disrespected and unworthy of your feelings.

HOW TO RESPOND TO INVALIDATION

When you suppress your own desires, and act according to another's will, you're allowing that person to control your thoughts and actions. After experiencing a person's repeated invalidation, you begin to doubt yourself. This is unfortunate, but you hold the solution within you.

Once more, when someone rejects, ignores, judges, mocks, teases, or diminishes how another feels, it's considered *invalidation*. When one party continually invalidates another, it's *chronic invalidation,* which experts consider one of the most devastating forms of verbal abuse.

If you're in a relationship in which you feel you're being constantly invalidated, there's a chance that the other party is a narcissist. A narcissist is known to use invalidation as a tactic to gain control of another and attain power. Especially in more extreme instances, this is his or her sole motivation and he or she will do whatever it takes to accomplish this objective. Once you understand this, you'll realize that there's no reasoning with this person, for whom all communication is a game about control.

As an adult, however, you must realize you always have choices. And for your self-preservation, it's vital you establish clear boundaries of what you will and won't accept. Remember, you should never have to do anything against your will or conscience for another person's acceptance.

Invalidation is a form of psychological attack. In response, you can defend yourself or withdraw. Repeated withdrawal can destroy your confidence and lead you to feelings of powerlessness and depression. At the same time, going on the offensive can escalate the problem as well as put you in the position of trying to change another as it threatens your safety.

A more effective approach is to express your feelings when you believe you've been invalidated, by simply responding "I feel invalidated" or "I feel judged" or any concise statement regarding what feelings you're experiencing. This is also a more rational answer than counter-attacking.

The other person's response to your emotional honesty will indicate how much he or she respects you and cares about your feelings. Or it can expose how much he or she is trying to change or control you, which is often revealed by his or her defensiveness or indifference.

His or her response will help you make decisions that are in your best interest. It would be beneficial at this point to evaluate your personal standards in practicing tolerance and kindness. These are always up for revision. You can become more tolerant and leave yourself vulnerable to repeated invalidation or you can *raise the bar* in deciding you won't accept this show of disrespect. Choose wisely. Your standards will establish future boundaries of behaviors you will or won't accept from this individual.

If you're in the early stages of a casual relationship, it's good to keep it casual until you determine if he or she respects you and cares about your feelings. This is a time to keep your standards high, so you can be selective in choosing whether to remain in the relationship and trust him or her enough to allow intimacy. Otherwise, you may learn to regret your choice.

If you're already involved with a *significant other* or mate and you continually feel invalidated, you can suggest counseling, but caution is in order. If the other party is repeatedly invalidating you, he or she may use the same manipulative tactics to convince a professional that the problem is yours. If the invalidating person is a narcissist, that individual is already an expert manipulator and may be successful implementing his or her ploy.

A counselor who's savvy to this form of invalidation may catch a controlling person *in the act*, and call him or her on it. The narcissist is likely to respond out of defensiveness, reject the confrontation out of hand, and deny any responsibility in creating this serious communication problem.

Like other efforts to control another person this pattern of verbal abuse can transition into the perpetration of domestic violence that can be physical and/or sexual and creates a life-threatening environment for a woman, as well as her offspring. Sometimes the only option is escape, which you should plan in private or with intimate family and friends, and well in advance, if possible. Once more, the Domestic Violence Hotline is 1-800-799-SAFE, (7233). If you're in imminent danger, call 911.

CHANGE

FINDING JOY IN THE ACCEPTANCE OF CHANGE

As we can observe in nature, change is a continuous part of life. It can be a natural transition or sudden transformation. Only the human species labels the inevitable process of change as inherently good or bad. In assessing the meaning of a particular change, we possess the unique ability to *reason*, which can be hindered by our emotional limitations. But when we expand our awareness of the potential value of change, we realize it's limitless, especially as we apply our gratitude and faith—not necessarily from a religious perspective, but from our sense that we're evolving.

If someone holds a very strong belief, he or she may not be able to accept any evidence that works against it, since that would create an intense feeling of discomfort. Since it's important to protect his or her belief, the individual may ignore and deny anything that conflicts with it.

Let's say a man suddenly tells his wife that he doesn't love her anymore and further, he's going to leave her. She may have sensed this at a barely conscious level for a while before he confronts her with the truth of his loss of affection for her, but she resists admitting this to herself, because it's too painful for her to accept. When he finally confronts her with this reality, she finds it virtually impossible to believe, at least at first, because she's held on so tight to her belief that he loves her—indeed as though her life depends on it, when in fact she's chosen to give it this importance.

If this same woman accepted the inevitability of change since the onset of her relationship with her husband—and with this the possibility that one day he might no longer care for her—she might have been more proactive in developing her own interests. If she realized in noticing certain clues, such as his increasing lack of attention, that he seemed to be losing his attraction to her, she would have been more prepared for his behavior and could have adjusted to it by becoming more independent—emotionally, in her daily activities, and financially. She might have taken a job she enjoyed. Her actions could then result in one of two outcomes: 1) the man's feelings could be rekindled when he sees that she's growing or 2) he may still want to leave. Either way, she's become more self-reliant, she's developed more self-esteem, and she may realize that she'll actually be happier on her own.

Even in the best relationships, people sometimes grow apart. It's far less disturbing for both parties to accept the breakup as a natural outcome of the effects of life changes, rather than blaming one another. Many couples separate amicably, which saves them and any children involved from the potential *devastation* of pain based on the largely unnecessary drama and agitation of divorce.

In the above scenario the woman's actions are in response to the man's, but this isn't the only standard. Ideally, in a loving relationship a woman and a man (or a woman and a woman) discuss each partner's rights to develop his or her own interests and serve his or her own needs, as long as it doesn't undermine their shared responsibilities as well as their mutual respect and care for one another. Either one can initiate independent action with some thoughtful discussion and support from the other. If their actions lead to their growing in separate directions, it's healthier to acknowledge the reality than to fight one another as a result of its natural occurrence.

Yes, it can be sad, but out of respect for the original relationship, separation doesn't need to bring about a war of mutual denunciation. While unfortunately a lawsuit is a prevalent manner in which couples divorce, it's not the most honorable and considerate way to bring about change, especially when each party knows in his or her heart *it's over*. In contrast, while it's relatively rare, two individuals can celebrate together their shared memories, the bittersweet melancholy of loss, and even the approaching adventure of change. This demands the wisdom and maturity of each individual. And it requires authenticity.

When any major change occurs that we find difficult to accept, we may be inclined to see this change as negative or tragic. But this does a disservice to the respect and wonder that all change warrants, particularly when it's beyond our full comprehension. For instance, if a transition is from life to death, we can celebrate the beauty of life just as we mourn its loss and we can choose to accept the credible theory that death is transcendence from life to another dimension of expanded consciousness.

LEARNING FROM THE PAST TO EFFECT POSITIVE CHANGE

We can learn from our past experience. And when we apply our new awareness to our current actions, we can evolve into increasingly self-reliant, authentic, and as a result happy individuals.

But if we don't consciously practice what we've learned, we tend to rely on the same old ways of doing things, and repeatedly run up against the same challenges. Expecting varied results for identical action is nonsense. If this pattern sounds familiar to you, it's quite possible you're among the multitude of people who are reluctant to change, out of fear of the unknown and the possibility of failure.

One of the biggest changes I've ever made was deciding to become an independent writer who advocates women's advancement. It was scary at first, to say the least, because the future was impossible to predict, and it seemed all up to me to determine my own success— or my failure. Looking back, while I've faced many obstacles, and tripped over some, I've kept moving forward with resolve and a wavering belief in myself, despite any evidence to the contrary. Now I can honestly say that every day has been an adventure in learning how to develop new skills and conquer my own reticence. I wouldn't trade my life experience for anything in the world.

I can say from firsthand experience that it's OK to look at past failures, rejections and mistakes, when we use the knowledge and wisdom we've gained from them to improve our actions and generate better results. It's not OK when we dwell on the past, immobilized by fear, and hold on to toxic relationships, as well as our own habits and behaviors that are harmful to our health, wellbeing, self-reliance, happiness, and personal evolution.

It's only when we conquer our reluctance to change and try new approaches to challenges that we begin to find viable new solutions. In the process—if we're really paying attention to our own needs and desires instead of blindly fulfilling the expectations of others— we can begin to self-actualize and make true progress in achieving results that work for us.

This also enables us to be of service to others, since it's ultimately through self-love and self-respect that we have something of value to share with others, especially our loved ones, who need our genuine care, emotional support, and assistance.

We live in a symbiotic world. While we each strive to be as self-sufficient as possible, we rely on one another for life and sustenance. With this in mind, we only reach our full potential when together we create a balance of give and take. As we empower ourselves to share our compassion with others, in turn we receive the abundance that love has to offer.

THE CHANGING NATURE
OF FRIENDSHIP

When a friendship is slipping away you can feel the loss inside. You've invested time with this person, you've shared confidences, and you've been through good times and bad together.

But now your friend doesn't return your calls. He or she doesn't have time to spend with you and may offer a *rational* reason, but you sense it's just an excuse. Something is amiss. And you have a nagging suspicion that you've done something wrong. But what is it?

Perhaps you haven't done anything to offend or hurt your friend. Before you torture yourself with guilt and regret over some unknown transgression, ask yourself a few questions:

- While you once had similar values, have they changed over time?
- Do your lifestyles have less in common than when you first met?
- Has your friend been supportive during recent contacts?
- Are you enjoying your time together, or is your pleasure forced?
- Does your friend ever undermine you or seem to sabotage you?
- Do you have doubts that you can trust your friend?

If your answer is *yes* to any or all of the above questions, your next step is to decide if you want to continue your friendship. It doesn't seem to be a priority to your friend lately. Is it worth your doubts and discomfort? Do you really want to find out why this distancing has occurred and to try to close the gap or deep inside do you want to let go?

Here are some things to consider: 1) Time and distance can change things: this is life's natural course. While you may want to hold onto the past, it isn't always possible or even recommended; 2) Your friend may be going through some rough times and experiencing difficulty sharing them with you; 3) Your friend may in fact be disturbed by something you've said or done, or 4) You and your friend have developed separate values.

If your soul searching leads you to decide the friendship could be worth saving, then it's up to you to swallow your pride and ask your friend if something's wrong. This may not be easy, because you don't know in advance the outcome of your discussion. Emotions can become heated. But hostility isn't necessary, at least not on your side of things, if you make up your mind to approach matters with fairness. Be ready to listen. And be prepared to apologize if your friend has a valid complaint.

The worst thing that can happen as a result of your well-intentioned confrontation is you won't be able to resolve the conflict and you'll part estranged. But if you try to maintain peace this isn't likely to happen. You can agree to disagree, and decide to end your relationship on it previous terms. This can be more satisfying than forever wondering what went wrong.

But there's a potential reward if you approach a true friend with genuine care and concern: Your conversation just might bring a new level of mutual understanding, and make the bond between you stronger than before. This can make reaching out more than worth the effort as well as the possibility of embarrassment. Relationships that have weathered storms through authentic communication can be satisfying because they're meaningful: You stretched yourself to your limit of vulnerability to get to the truth and save your mutual care, trust and respect.

There's just one caveat: resist the temptation to force a positive outcome. Your dignity and your friend's are at stake. Respect this and things will be resolved with integrity.

CHANGES BEYOND OUR CONTROL

H ow do we maintain even a modicum of control in our culture of rapid technological and social change? Especially as women who are often underpaid, overworked, and on our own—trying to balance our work and personal lives—we find little comfort in the platitude "We're all in the same boat" because we know some of us are in smaller boats than others. We're told that if we all work together we can accomplish anything. We want to believe this—and we may do our best to help make something that seems impossible happen—but the task can seem overwhelming.

Things happen fast these days—so fast they seem to spin out of control without warning: we lose our jobs or we're faced with unexpected medical bills. Suddenly we lose a chunk of our life savings; that is, if we have one. As we bang our heads against the wall— chiding ourselves with w*oulda coulda, shoulda*—we conclude that whatever disaster we're facing was at least largely beyond our control. We can rant against the injustice. But our righteous rage doesn't bring our hard-earned money back.

Part of change is loss, and financial loss can be hurtful. In fact any loss can be devastating. If it's a result of our ignorance or carelessness, we learn from the experience and start over with more knowledge. But when anything happens beyond our control, our healthiest emotional response is to let it go.

Even if we lose *everything*, we still have our inner selves, including our values and resources. This may seem like small consolation, but we each have influence through our authentic self-expression, in good times and not so good. There's power in this realization. Our response to the inevitable doesn't necessarily destroy us. It can actually strengthen us when we use our new knowledge to rebuild our lives, which may not be as difficult as we expect, since we're starting over with our acquired experience.

Much of the awareness that we're not completely in control is in respect to other people. The term *controlling person* can bring a distinct image to mind of a bullying individual who insists on controlling others in getting his or her own way. But we're entitled to listen to our inner voice when it calls out *foul* in response to someone's efforts to undermine our reality. And we can enforce our objections with a simple *no*.

In fact, despite others' efforts to demoralize us, we are 100% responsible for our own choices. As we accept responsibility for our lives, we realize we have a right to voice our feelings, preferences, and beliefs. We can assert ourselves in a calm manner. We can even use humor to detonate animosity as we establish personal boundaries. This awareness is a liberating experience. It's freedom we can implement at will on a personal level.

Being *out of control* is a matter of degree. Plus, the question is: Who's control—our own or someone else's? In respecting our own boundaries we must respect others' as well. Hopefully, we don't become that mean-spirited bully, because we realize it's inhumane and we recognize the futility of trying to control others. No one can predict the future. Still, we try to remain flexible and prepare ourselves for any eventuality. Actually, women, including those who experience emotional trauma, often learn to use deep reservoirs of strength to deal with life's surprises—both big and small.

The world is an unpredictable place. How do we prepare for the unexpected? Our skills in communication play a crucial role: I advocate expressing courage, kindness, and humor, whenever possible. Then, if we collide with fate, we stand a good chance to prevail and even triumph. And we may gain a good story to tell— perhaps inspiring others.

As women, we each have a voice. And we all have choices. How we use these gifts is up to us. Our experiences—without labels of good or bad—can strengthen us and enhance our lives as we dream, plan and work toward our goals. While some things happen outside our control, we can object to unacceptable behavior. Or if someone brings us joy, we can say "I love you" out loud, in a whisper or with a smile.

ADAPTATION: YOUR
KEY TO SUCCESS

I f we could anticipate the outcomes of our actions, we could become wildly successful in all our endeavors, immensely wealthy, and ecstatic with our romantic relationships. But, though some of us devote a lifetime analyzing the market, testing products, and researching every facet of life to predict positive outcomes, no one has been able to master looking into the future since it never stands still. The only thing permanent is change.

We can increase the odds of ensuring our relative success by applying reason and educated guesses, calculating the odds, and using our gut instincts, but even these methods aren't infallible. Despite our best efforts at prediction the future is unfathomable. The only way we can survive and possibly succeed is to learn to adapt to life's inherent change.

Although we're the only life form on the planet with the ability to reason, let's be real. How many of us use our capacity for reason to make every small decision in life, or even a large one? We don't have time. Besides, it would drive us bonkers. At the same time, many of us are frazzled in trying to keep up with every little change or *advancement* that life throws our way: We think we must wear the latest fashions, buy the most cutting-edge technology, and follow every passing fad—all so that we don't appear behind the times to our peers. While impulse buying may boost our morale, habitual collecting of clothing, gadgets, etc. can lead to financial disaster—at least it can greatly interfere with our freedom to follow our passion and live on our terms.

Most of us alter the tactics we use in our approach to life in order to keep things interesting—avoiding the boredom that occurs when we resist change. But before we deplete our energy and run our finances amuck, we must determine what's most important to our survival. Fads and material trinkets are low on the list. First, we must prioritize our values. What do we want and—even more significant—what do we need most?

Adapting to changes that come naturally with time are generally more relevant to our survival than manmade changes, which often involve planned obsolescence. The good news is that any change—no matter how serious or daunting it seems on the surface—carries potential for the fun and exhilaration of a new adventure. It depends entirely on our attitude: If it's one of acceptance, curiosity, and an *I got this* point of view, we can turn potential problems into opportunities and achieve far more than we expect.

A *can do* attitude is intrinsic to self-sufficiency—the key to survival for every woman and every man. In a nutshell, this means being able to adapt to the barrage of changes that can affect our lives, including our financial resources. Adaptation is crucial if we remain single and rely solely on ourselves to provide the resources to subsist. If we're married it's wise to work out financial plans with our mate, but the best-laid plans are subject to change, such as a spouse's loss of work, divorce, illness, or death.

These are ways women can prepare to adapt to change:

- Cultivate a skill, obtain an education, in order to be employable. This is not a one-time achievement, but an ongoing process that demands continual updating to adapt to the changing market and maintain relevant qualifications.
- Create a savings account and put some money aside on a regular basis. Don't touch it, unless there's an emergency and even then only use what's absolutely necessary.

- Network with women and men to learn where opportunities can be found at any given time. A meaningful referral can be invaluable.

If, despite your best efforts, you find yourself stagnant in your job, or unhappy in your marriage or relationship, it's important that you be honest about the fact that things aren't working in a productive and satisfactory way. This requires self-love and self-respect. To ignore something that's hurting you is to allow a stressful situation to undermine your health and wellbeing. Sadly, out of fear of the unknown, many of us remain in a downward spiral of toxic circumstances, reluctant to admit that we don't seem able to effectively manage its harmful influence.

Rather than put your head in the proverbial sand, you must recognize early that bouts of recurring stress signal the exact time and circumstance when it's most to your advantage to be adaptable and do all that's in your power to make a necessary change—turning it into a positive, life-affirming transition toward increased autonomy. Accepting this challenge is precisely what promotes your growth and empowerment.

We are not helpless and inept, although those afraid of our potential power might try to make us feel as though we are. It's time for all women to adapt, survive and succeed according to our needs, values and desires, instead of condemning ourselves to become submissive casualties of change.

INDEPENDENCE AND INTERDEPENDENCE

THE VALUE OF A FRIEND
AND HOW TO BE ONE

What quality do you value most in a friend? Whether you stop to think about it or answer off the top of your head, what comes to mind? You may or may not be surprised that whenever I ask a woman what she values most in a friend, the answer is often *honesty*.

Trust is important in even the most casual relationship. It becomes especially vital in a friendship, which is a state of mutual respect and support. Trustworthy friends are valuable beyond measure. If you have an honest friend, never take her or him for granted.

If you have more than one true friend, you are indeed fortunate. If on the other hand, you don't know anyone that you feel you can trust, you may want to start to think about how to make authentic friends, for they will enhance the quality of your life. Even if you find only one in your lifetime search, you've discovered a priceless ally.

But how do we *make* true friends? It's been said *to have a friend you must be one*. This isn't as easy as it may sound. It certainly doesn't happen overnight. As with anything worthwhile, it takes patience, acceptance, sensitivity—and perhaps most of all—trustworthiness.

It's a mistake to think of friends as people who help you get what you want. In fact, it's unethical. A real friend is someone you are grateful to know for his or her intrinsic value as a fellow human being. Perhaps the ideal friendship is one in which neither party ever asks a favor from the other—especially one that's difficult or painful for him or her to fulfill. It's best if you can enjoy your friend(s) as you maintain your independence—without putting your relationship to a test that can weaken the bond of trust. If you get down on your luck, any favors you might ask a friend should be in proportion to how your friend might help you without sustaining a loss that will cause him or her inconvenience, discomfort, or suffering.

On the other hand, if you feel like you couldn't rely on a particular person if there were a problem and one of you needed help, perhaps there are issues of reciprocity based on trust. If you have evidence there are trust concerns within your relationship, it's wise to be cautious in pursuing a stronger connection or tacitly agreeing to a friendship or romance.

You're never required to disclose your deepest and darkest secrets to someone, especially in order to prove your friendship. If you do, it's unfair to expect your friend to reciprocate. We're all entitled to privacy. If you have a strong compulsion to share something about yourself with a friend, be as certain as possible that you can trust that individual. If it's something unpleasant, why place the burden on your friend, or swear him or her to secrecy? Too many contingencies can add stress to any relationship.

At the same time, demonstrate your trustworthiness with your actions. Besides not betraying your friend's trust, it's wise not to betray a third party's secret or say something hurtful about that individual. Your friend will then have reason to wonder if you will do the same to him or her.

Trust is meant to create feelings of comfort and pleasure within a relationship, not to create a quagmire of secrets and issues that make both parties feel ill at ease—straining communication. Friendship also requires balance. If you show that you have an interest in someone and care about that individual's welfare by listening to his or her concerns with consideration—sometimes putting his or her needs before yours—a real friend will respond with actions that verify his or her care for you. This way you both nurture your relationship and help it continue to thrive.

If you and your friend disagree about an issue, it's unnecessary to fight—just respect one another's point of view. Talk about it if you must, but don't feel compelled to win an argument. Then nobody wins. It's not worth it at the cost of a friend.

True friendship is rewarding and life-sustaining. It brings joy, freedom, peace of mind, and dignity to each friend.

BUILDING RELATIONSHIPS WITH FRIENDSHIP POTENTIAL

Making genuine friends is different than meeting new contacts. Contacts can develop into friendships—but only under the right circumstances. It's wise to keep your values in order, or else you can lose established friends as well as potential ones:

Perhaps you've just moved to a new environment. Maybe you plan to network to get that dream job. You're determined to impress key people you meet. You think with some trepidation that you may be wise to put your friendships on hold while you *climb* your way to popularity and success.

Your real friends are your most valuable assets. But while true friends will be glad to help out, they won't want to feel used. Always put friendship first—and not for personal gain. Stay in touch with your friends, and show them you care. Anyone new you meet is at first a contact or acquaintance, possibly with the potential to become a friend.

If you've just moved to a different city, your friends are miles away. You've attended a cookout or two, but you aren't making much progress in forming new bonds. You wonder what's wrong. You wear a big smile. You have the gift of gab. You're savvy on most topics. Why aren't your listeners in awe of your conversation skills? First do some honest self-assessment, especially if you're noticing some glassy-eyed stares when you're speaking to virtual strangers.

Perhaps you're trying too hard to be *on*. In other words, you're struggling to impress your new contacts with your background, knowledge, or performance skills, but it's obvious to others that you're focused on yourself in your efforts to wow your target spectators. It doesn't matter how well you understand the facts regarding a particular subject; your audience realizes you have no interest in any response or interaction. Take heart, you're not alone in talking a bit too much, especially under pressure, real or imagined.

Put yourself in your listener's place. How many times have you tried to listen to someone who talks incessantly about himself or herself? My guess is that you felt frustrated, irritated, and possibly demoralized. As the speaker, allow your listener to speak often. If you're paying attention, you may learn something. Ask polite questions in a friendly tone. Then listen. When it's your turn to talk, let him or her know you heard what he or she said. If you want others to take notice of your words, it's vital that you engage them in conversation. This requires finding meaningful connections with them. It can only occur when individuals know their meaning is understood. It's up to you to establish your acceptance and empathy.

Networking usually alludes to making contacts within a business context, which has a somewhat more formal structure than making social contacts. At a networking event, the idea is to move from person to person with ease, connecting with other professionals in brief conversations to discover shared or complementary objectives. While this pattern can be intimidating, probably the biggest faux pas you can make is to gravitate to one person and stick like glue throughout the event, despite an implicit understanding among others that everyone is there to find new business opportunities and meet prospective clients—not to make a new best friend.

With practice, it becomes easier and more enjoyable to network and make new contacts. You can accumulate hundreds—even thousands—of contacts over time, whether you're networking at an event or online—or even better—experiencing both venues. Making new contacts is an accomplishment when you use an interactive approach that meaningful to both or all parties concerned.

You never know what relationship might develop with the next person you meet—perhaps a lifetime friendship, although this can't be forced. *Schmoozing* can actually undermine any attempt to connect. Remember mutual trust doesn't happen overnight. The key is to relax. Take one pleasant and stress-free step at a time.

DECLARING OUR
INTERDEPENDENCE

Our forefathers shared some uniquely selfless ideals in founding the U.S. We're proud of our independence and we value its abundance, even if our share is *modest*—a mild word in describing the standards of living some of us endure. A disturbing number of women are living on our own, without the support of a family or a stable job. Many of us struggle to support our children, without sufficient income, childcare, or healthcare. At this writing, more than half of all children in families headed by women live below the poverty line; two thirds of minimum wage earners are women; and one in seven women lives below the poverty line. In fact, for millions of women, our share of the nation's wealth is meager at best.

But we maintain our dignity. We can be proud of the courage we display in meeting enormous challenges on a daily basis. For the most part we're stoic and hold it all together with hope for a better future, if not for us, for our children. Our resilience, our tenacity, and our faith seem to have no bounds. We keep our heads held high, in part because we can't afford to do otherwise, since our neglect would cause our fragile world to fall apart.

There's a secret to our strength: We've learned firsthand that gratitude is the most empowering—and most humane—attitude we can take. We whistle in the dark to deny our fear of the night. We may dream of freedom from our earthly burdens, but we understand our societal challenges endow us with our humanity. And while most of us would like more financial independence, we may be looking ahead to years, decades, or generations of struggle, servitude, and dependence on others to live at subsistence level.

Thankfully, wherever we live on the globe, there's some reason to hope. We have nothing to be ashamed of if we're *working class*, which includes all ranks of people who serve others. Women who are working to make the world a little better place, or even just to survive another day, are doing our part in a world of *interdependence*— another way to express our reliance on one another. There's honor in this. It gives our lives purpose.

Those of us who do what we can to prevail and embrace our connection with others are contributing to a vast web of oneness. Our efforts at reaching out give us reason for pride tempered with humility. A sense of belonging emanates from the fact that we're doing our best to stand on our own two feet. While we're grateful we can trust in the decency of humanity enough to get by, we limit our requests for help to the times when we have needs of vital concern.

We can dream of more financial independence—even plan for it. But we stand the best chance at the joy of self-respect if we practice gratitude for the amazing labors of love among human beings. We are giving and taking in fulfillment of our capacity to care for one another. And as we practice our compassion globally, the potential for shared abundance continues to grow.

THE BEST TIME TO SEIZE OPPORTUNITY

O ur time is priceless. No matter who we are and regardless of our wealth, fame, prestige or lack thereof, we only have a limited amount of time on this earth, Time is even more valuable than money, because once it's lost there's no way we can regain it. The sooner we realize the value of time, the more likely we are to spend it in ways that are beneficial to us. But how do we decide what's good for us, or what will bring us happiness?

Before we decide to take an action that could waste our valuable time, it's essential that we look deep within ourselves to begin to understand what will give us joy—as distinguished from what others expect from us—because what we believe will make us happy can be immensely different from what our family and friends think we should do with our lives.

So first we must demand absolute honesty in our thinking. Each of us is the only one in the *driver's seat*, and no one else is entitled to make the decisions that determine the course of our life. This doesn't give us license to be selfish and disregard others' feelings. It doesn't sanction blowing all our money on a night of gambling, just because we think it's fun, regardless of the lasting consequences. A wise use of time is much like a wise use of money. And it's wise to invest both toward a fulfilling and meaningful future, rather than limit our thinking to immediate gratification.

Of course, we may want an ice-cream sundae on occasion, or that expensive designer handbag, and that's OK, but when we make a habit of spending much of our money on temporal luxuries, we may find we have nothing left at the end of the month for the necessities of life, like gasoline or rent. It's the same with time as with money. If we fritter our days and months away with little or no thought for the future, we lose time that we could use creating the best possible lives for ourselves.

Especially when we're young, we may believe we have forever to worry about how we spend our time, or how our actions impact the rest of our lives. But our youth is the perfect time to think about what will make us happy in the long term, and begin to do something about it. When we're young we're surrounded by opportunities, many of which won't wait for us forever. While the phrase *it's never too late* holds a great deal of truth it can be more difficult to accomplish important goals when we postpone them, and besides, we can never regain the time we lost in evading responsibility.

Do you remember a time when you watched an opportunity slip away? If so, how did it make you feel? I don't think I'm alone when I say I've lost opportunities. And I have felt some regret for not taking action about something I cared about when the time was right.

No one else can tell you what the best actions are when you're faced with a particular opportunity, because they're different for each of us, but you won't know either, until you focus on what is meaningful for you that will likely still be meaningful for you tomorrow and the next day. You can't predict the future, because things always change. But you must develop trust in yourself and be true to yourself in making the best possible choice at any given moment.

It's not advantageous to limit yourself to boring predictable choices to try to avoid any risk. Some risk is unavoidable, especially if you want to live your life fully rather than merely exist. Determine whether a potential opportunity is based on a value, goal, or purpose that rouses your passion and excitement. Consider what will hold your attention for an extended period of time and what holds the most ultimate promise for a better future.

Wherever you are in life, and whatever your age, opportunities are to be seized upon; that is, if they're real. If one seems too good to be true, it's wise to investigate it, but don't let one slip away if it's something you really want and seems within your grasp—even it if requires time and work to attain it. The best things in life are worth the effort it takes to achieve them. And true happiness comes from the self-respect we feel when we're accountable for our choices.

The real fun and excitement is the adventure of pursuing our dreams—not just the rest stops along the way. If you keep your eyes open for opportunities that are significant to you—and put your heartfelt enthusiasm into seeking them—you'll discover they're all around you. Some people call them coincidences, luck, or fate. Others call them miracles.

Regardless of the sources of opportunities that could change your life, they're often most satisfying and worthy of your appreciation when you take an active and selective part in making them happen.

THE BLIND JUSTICE OF
LOVE AND BALANCE

T he best relationships are always built on mutual trust and respect. Healthy relationships can't survive, let alone thrive, without the respect that's built on consistent honesty. Both parties are equally responsible for creating trust and communicating their truth in an upfront manner, without hidden agendas or manipulation to gain an unfair advantage.

The truth can mean more than one thing: 1) It can reflect the outlook, feelings, and opinions of someone from his or her own perspective, which is often subjective and based on bias; or 2) it can represent the truth as an objective manifestation of reality, which can be difficult or impossible for one person to grasp without the influence of his or her limiting perception.

Open and honest communication means each party discusses his or her feelings and perspectives without judgment or schemes to *win* over the other. Each person realizes that that he or she doesn't have a corner on the truth. Through talking with respect and compassion for one another, they reach an understanding of the fairest resolution to their separate views, while taking into consideration each person's needs for validation and wellbeing.

If one loved one, friend, or partner is continually submitting to the other's paradigm of what is real or false, right or wrong, good or bad, that individual is likely being manipulated by a self-serving individual for his or her own benefit. This represents an unbalanced relationship in which the submissive partner is not being treated as an equal or enjoying the respect she or he deserves, but is rather under the control of a bully, a narcissist, or an abuser—quite possibly all three.

As humans, we are all multifaceted beings, with the intrinsic right to be heard—to have our needs for acceptance, validation and respect acknowledged, especially by those who claim to care about us. And we each want to be free to make our own choices without unwarranted influence.

Attempting to control another individual and to indoctrinate her or him with a belittling concept of her- or himself is a serious form of abuse, analogous to enslaving that person with mental and emotional trickery.

A loving relationship allows space for each person to enjoy the freedom of self-expression as long as he or she is not undermining the other party's inherent rights or abusing her or his emotional needs.

When you first meet someone it's impossible to know that person completely; in fact, you can never totally understand another, since you haven't lived his or her life. So how do you move forward, without taking on the risk of being the subject of someone's unwitting or intentional actions to hurt you and do personal harm? To try to avoid all risk is to hide from the potential joys of life. But you can still minimize your chance of becoming a victim to a dishonest *user*, who only has his or her best interests in mind.

Since we're all complicated, none of us can ever know all there is to know everything about another individual, but you always have a choice any time you meet a fellow human being: you can allow mistrust to guide you or try to keep an open mind and a willingness to express yourself with honesty.

While this doesn't mean you're required to tell your life story duing your first encounter with someone, it does imply that you should be truthful about our thoughts, interests, needs, and values, and listen to that person with the same respect that you wish from him or her.

From this beginning of mutual cooperation, a relationship can grow. You can assert your rights and boundaries and allow that person to do the same. If the friendship or love continues to grow, you're' on the right track to shared trust, a relationship between equals, and genuine happiness. But if your instincts tell you the other person's responses seem like *red flags*—signaling you that 1) your trust is likely to be betrayed and/or 2) your safety and wellbeing are at risk—it's most likely time to summon the courage to walk away with your mind, body, and spirit still intact.

WHO'S IN CHARGE OF YOUR DESTINY?

I hope as you're reading this you're thinking to yourself, "I'm in charge of my destiny." I'm not saying you don't ever need others to guide you and help you along on your journey. Nor am I implying that there is no universal force if not determining at least influencing your fate. But I do believe that God—or a Creative Force—gives us the gift of free will. Whatever your beliefs, you deserve your self-love. So believe in yourself and trust yourself enough to claim the right to make your own choices, especially the most important ones, including:

- What do you value most?
- What do you want to do with your life?
- How do you want to share your love?
- What is your greatest life purpose?

No one else has the right to make these choices for you. Your life choices are a privilege and a blessing and carry deep personal significance. They belong to you and you alone.

Yes, sometimes choices can seem scary. Once we make decisions that will determine our destiny we must accept responsibility for them, and that can feel overwhelming. But when we think about it, if we're really making choices for ourselves—without outside pressure or influence—the choices that will awaken our happiness are also the most responsible because they will free us to share our unique gifts—along with our love and gratitude—with openness and genuine pleasure. Conversely, we're actually entitled to be happy as long as we accept responsibility for our choices.

But there's another side to this issue: At the same time we're each entitled to make our own choices, we're not entitled to sit back and wait for someone to make us happy. Our happiness is our purpose and responsibility.

If you believe you've relinquished your right to determine your destiny more than you care to admit, it's time to love yourself more, believe in yourself more, and trust yourself more every day of your life, starting today. When you do, you'll begin to discover you can share yourself more freely from you heart, because you want to, not because you must. When you love yourself, it's so much easier to love your friends, your family, and everyone you meet—by choice, not mandate.

The *other*s in our lives are not supposed to be our burden and they don't want to be. They want the freedom and dignity to make their own choices, just as we do. We're not entitled to expect them to love us out of a sense of duty. Nor do we have the right to make their decisions for them.

There's a saying that we all get older, but maturity is optional. Unfortunately, there's truth in this. People are born to grow and evolve, but some resist personal growth all or most of our lives out of a lack of confidence or dread of adverse consequences. Wisdom only comes with experience and we can't fully experience life without some willingness to be vulnerable in exploring our human potential.

Of course, as children we're not ready to accept full responsibility for ourselves. It's in large part the responsibility of our parents and other adults in our lives to provide us with a secure and happy childhood, at least as much as is possible. But as children, we also need preparation for adulthood, so we can become independent and make good choices—our choices. This will never happen if adults don't encourage us to become autonomous, at the same time letting us know we're loved and trusted.

Let's release whatever happened to us—especially as

children—that's sabotaged our self-assurance. Let's forgive our loved ones for being human. We can make the choice to model a code of kindness and respect for others, despite what may be the blaming, meddling, or bullying habits of anyone else in our lives. We're free to begin this moment, if for no other reason than to find peace of mind. It could be the best choice we ever make.

Beyond this, perhaps we can inspire those we love to do the same. But if someone we know just doesn't seem to *get it*, it's not our job to coerce him or her. This is a lesson in wisdom that's essential we learn for ourselves.

LEARNING TO TRUST YOURSELF

Before we're fully adult—even before our preteens—we begin to realize that we can't rely on others to serve all our needs. It's healthy to acknowledge this and take pleasure and pride in becoming more independent. While no man or woman is an *island*, it's imperative that we can trust ourselves to become effectively autonomous in providing for our livelihood as well as setting boundaries for our protection.

While many women attend public or private school, at least through most of high school, and some of us go to college or technical school, a curriculum is meaningless unless we want to learn. Still, usually following some form of education, many of us find work to support ourselves and perhaps our families. The more motivated we are to succeed in making a living that provides a productive life and even fulfills our passion, the more likely we'll adapt to adult life as self-sufficient—and happy—individuals.

For women, the pressure to marry can undermine our path toward personal growth if we allow it. While marriage is not inherently detrimental to a woman's advancement toward her full potential, it can influence her to play a secondary role to her husband, remaining at home without a compelling purpose, while he assumes the traditional role of *provider*. Having children can create a sense of purpose that's very real, but in today's culture offspring are not considered mandatory to marriage—but rather a personal choice. Besides, focusing on children likely contributes to their development more than their mother's. Too often, women put everyone else's needs before their own, and feel depleted and undervalued as a result.

Whether you're married or single, it's critical that you develop your own sense of self-esteem that's not dependent on the positions or status of your family— which could include yours, your parents' or your husband's parents—because this has little or nothing to do with the development of your character, which is all about learning to trust yourself as a fully functioning female who is capable of acting out of your own free will. Below are some steps that can help you to gain confidence in expressing your true self, without shame or apology:

- Forgive yourself. Put regrets and unhappy memories in the past where they belong. You've learned from these experiences and now it's time to move forward.
- Develop awareness of your thoughts and feelings. Express them with assertiveness and consideration for others' feelings, too.
- Establish your standards and values and then do your best to follow them every day. Refuse to compromise your ethical code.
- Practice integrity, which means your actions are consistent with your words whether or not anyone is watching.
- Make commitments to yourself and others. Keep them. You can start small. For example, offer to do something kind for someone and then follow through.
- Speak with kindness to yourself. Stay busy with enjoyable esteem-building tasks to block out negative voices in your mind.
- Don't try to be perfect, just be real. Accept your humanity. Your need for self-trust is the knowledge that you can survive, prevail and succeed on your terms beyond any obstacle to your progress.
- Trust your instincts. If someone's negative behavior seems to be trying to tell you something—especially if it's ongoing— examine your feelings, and listen to your intuition that's trying to protect you.
- Don't lie to yourself about any negative feedback you receive from the universe, including your relationships. It can help

to keep a journal to discover recurring patterns in your own and others' behavior. Otherwise you may remain in a state of denial, fearful to confront a problem, or unwilling to leave an unhealthy situation.

- Don't try to control everything and everyone, so that you can feel safe. The only behavior you can control is your own. While you can be assertive in telling someone when he or she is hurting you, or asking what the problem is that's causing him or her to disrespect you, you can't effectively tell him or her how to behave. Sometimes walking away is preferable to confrontation. There's a huge difference between simply giving up and realizing that you've had enough.

- Finish what you start. Completing what you plan to do is a big step toward self-trust and resulting self-confidence. But there's an exception to this advice: Sometimes you may decide that it's useful to experiment, but in doing so, you don't get the results you want. This is a learning experience. Accept it without drama and don't repeat the same action to get different results. Use your new knowledge to figure out another more successful approach to reaching your objectives.

- Trust yourself to make your own decisions, instead of relying on others' advice. Sometimes people ask for advice because they think they should get a variety of opinions even though they expect some will be negative. While *polling* or *testing* may be advisable in some impersonal forums, such as business, don't get in the habit of doing this when it adversely affects your personal life decisions. You're accountable for making the right choices. First and foremost, listen to your authentic inner voice.

- Make a list of your many strengths, positive traits, and admirable qualities. Refer to this at times when you self-esteem is low.

- Nurture yourself. Give yourself time to play and relax. Make taking care of yourself your number one priority, so you have energy to share your joy with others. Meditation, which is basically clearing your mind, can be helpful.

- Stop being self-deprecating. This can be a tough one. Often people will say, "She has a wonderful self-deprecating sense of humor." While this can be a very likable trait, it's always a two-edged sword, because others will usually treat you with the same level of respect that you seem to have for yourself. In fact, a more selfish or narcissistic man or woman will often use your expressed weakness against you, to undermine your confidence—thereby gaining control of his or her relationship with you.

- Stay clear of people who undercut your self-sufficiency. While it may not be possible to completely avoid others who tend to demoralize you, you can give them a wide berth, and take their negative comments with a grain of salt. More often than not, they're reflecting their own lack of self–worth. They may be jealous of your proficiency and progress toward your goals. If someone you believe is a true friend keeps blocking productive communication with their negativity, it may be worthwhile to initiate a calm, non-blaming, win-win discussion of your feelings. But be aware that sometimes you can actually play into the hands of a *closet opponent* by bringing up a problem that they won't admit exists in an attempt to make you believe that you're overreacting to a meaningless incident from a *delusional* perspective.

These suggestions should be helpful along your journey toward your most authentic and best self, which are one and the same.

How Women Can Celebrate Independence

Both men and women celebrate Independence Day on July 4 in the U.S. Citizens in many other countries observe a special day of achieving sovereignty as well. But in most locales there are not-so-subtle differences between how women commonly observe freedom in contrast to men. One discrepancy—at least in western cultures—is that women might clean the dishes after the holiday barbecue while men watch sports on TV. While each gender is likely bonding among themselves in these ritual practices, we rarely if ever see the situation reversed—at least not in *traditional* families.

I suppose we could go on strike, insisting that men do the clean up while we go to the movies. But many of us tell ourselves it's not that important that we have our way in such *trivial* matters. We'd rather keep peace than cause an argument. But how many compromises are we required to make in order to keep an inherently unfair status quo intact? And just how are we to celebrate our freedom and autonomy if we live in more-or-less subservient rolls, not just at home but in the office as well?

First, we can pause to think just how far we've progressed in attaining our equality to men in every aspect of our lives. If that progress has been less than we had hoped—since yesterday or a year ago or even since we were girls—we can focus on exactly how we can continue to advance in bringing more justice and balance into our lives on a public and personal level. Here are a few suggestions concerning how we can become more independent:

- Assert our desires more in all our relationships. This doesn't mean expressing anger or aggression but simply stating our wants and needs—openly, directly, and with confidence.
- Express our values, thoughts and beliefs without apology. At the same time, we can be open to others' ideas when they are different than ours, respecting their freedom as much as our own.
- Love ourselves enough to value our rights to "life, liberty and the pursuit of happiness" and to protect those rights in daily practice, setting limits before they are threatened.
- Defend women's rights to liberty and equality when we vote.
- Show compassion for other women and children—especially those underserved—by coming to their aid and defense in public forums.

Real peace is based on justice and the compassion that secures it, not violence. We've been courageous for centuries in significant selfless ways. It's time to take our rightful place as leaders in creating a sustainable future for our loved ones, our country, and the world.

WHEN YOUR EGO IS IN CONTROL, YOU'RE NOT

An ego is not necessarily a good or bad thing. The word *ego* was originally Latin meaning *I*. We all need a healthy ego to survive and even thrive. But while other personality attributes are sometimes rated on a scale from 1 to 10, with 10 being the highest rating, an ideal ego reflects a balance of self-serving traits with merits that tend to be more selfless. For example, a 5, 6 or 7 on a scale of 10 can be considered optimal in rating a healthy ego, while a 10 is over the top—and likely represents an egoist or *narcissist*.

A 10 rating is detrimental to our best interests, because when the ego takes control of our every move, we actually become slaves to its demands. Not only this, but an overly egotistical disposition can make us intolerable to others. Of course this isn't you, but almost all of us have experienced watching a friend's eyes glaze over when we're talking—and if we're good at picking up cues—we realize that we've been running on a bit about our accomplishments and good fortune. Even if listeners are too kind to tell us to our face, when we monopolize conversations by talking about ourselves in glowing terms, they may be bored and possibly offended.

Here are a few self-checks to see whether your ego is taking control or if the *real you* is in charge:

The 100% unfiltered ego:

- Needs to be right all the time. Is incapable of an apology or admission of a mistake.

- Needs to be the best. It's more important to win than to play the game with fairness.
- Is easily offended. Thus relationships are fragile and easily broken.
- Is losing sight of his or her inner self—sometimes called a conscience or a soul. Deep inside he or she feels afraid, worried, depressed, or angry due to a loss of authentic self-esteem and peace of mind.

The healthy ego:

- Is open-minded and more concerned about learning from experience than being right or wrong. Keeps a sense of humor, admits mistakes, and continues to advance at her or his own pace.
- Competes only with her- or himself in working on self-improvement. Doesn't get involved in petty comparisons with others. Likes to help others succeed and is happy for their achievements.
- Stands up for her- or himself with assertiveness when important boundaries are crossed, but let's go of minor offenses. More concerned with a win-win outcome than *proving* superiority and perfection—an impossible task.
- Is self-aware and at peace with her or his inner growth, because it aligns with her or his values, integrity, and potential for happiness.

Examples of female unconstrained 100% narcissists are rare. But it seems as women we're more pressured all the time to be at the top of our game in every facet of our lives. This can result in our developing the compulsion to try to be flawless—an impossible objective and an unhealthy aspect of perfectionism.

So if your ego seems a little tarnished—from trying to maintain an image that conflicts with the remarkable human being hidden inside you—a little *auto correct* will set things right, allowing your authentic self to shine.

HOW TO STAND UP TO EXPLOITATION

As women, we often find it difficult to say how we feel. When someone hurts our feelings, we *suck it up* or *turn the other cheek,* making excuses for the person who's undermined us—telling ourselves they didn't really mean it. We're in denial. Or we decide it's not worth the effort to call someone out for disrespectful behavior.

We must stop enabling another's rudeness, insensitivity, and cruelty—and the sooner the better. It's critical to our peace of mind, our self-respect and even our health and safety that we establish limits between what we will and will not tolerate. Otherwise our passive acceptance of another's cruel behavior will signal that individual that he or she can repeat it without any appropriate consequences in response.

Take a moment to think about how and when you give others permission to treat you with disrespect. A particular person or event may come to mind. Or you may be able to think of several people you know that you'd like to give a piece of your mind, but you don't like confrontation. Others know this from the clues you give. The bullies in particular will take advantage of you time after time, if you let them. Even those who treat others with respect may overlook your right to considerate treatment, because they don't see your value—especially when you're self-effacing.

The phenomenon of men taking unfair advantage of their power over women is blatantly evident today. While it's disturbing, it offers us the opportunity to apply all our reserves of courage and integrity to put a stop to emotional, physical and sexual assault, abuse and harassment in all of its ugly forms—from verbal abuse and other offensive behaviors to rape, domestic violence and human trafficking. Women's support for one another is crucial in this global endeavor. When one of us becomes actively involved in resisting brutality we all move forward in a unified effort to replace cruelty and violence with reason, compassion, justice and ultimate peace.

While it's important to report any unlawful breach of women's rights by men or women, it's even more effective to stop invasive and inappropriate acts of aggression against us before they start, whenever possible. Ideally, as women become more financially independent we begin to carry more clout in our struggle for human liberties. But women's advancement has proven to be a huge challenge within our patriarchal culture. Although we're gaining momentum, tenacious effort will continue to be mandatory in freeing ourselves from pervasive exploitation.

Each of us must prioritize expressing our rights to humane treatment above our valid feelings of fear that are based on our economic dependence, our vulnerability, and our dispositions toward compassion. This requires raw courage, which we're progressively flexing in the face of intimidation. For many of us, it means breaking a lifetime pattern of excusing men for their unfeeling conduct toward us. But, in order to change, we're wise to avoid an uncontrolled response that might further endanger us.

We must simply make our feelings known in a civil but firm manner—not just with men, but with other women as well. When we stand up for ourselves every time someone attempts to cross our boundaries, we're teaching him or her to respect us as human beings, equal in every way to everyone else on the planet. It's best to begin this practice at the beginning of any relationship. While it may seem too late to expect those we've known for months or years to begin to treat us with respect, it's worth an earnest try.

If you're responding to a verbal affront, telling a man or woman how you feel doesn't necessitate fighting, yelling or screaming.

You're not obliged to say something hateful in return to someone's callousness. Limit your observation to expressing your feelings, instead of calling the other person a jerk, a *pervert* or whatever comes to mind (regardless of how appropriate the label might seem at the time). You can simply say, "That hurts me," or "I feel disrespected." Then—and only then— you can stop, listen and watch for that person's reaction.

If he or she tells you that you're 1) overreacting, 2) crazy, 3) silly, 4) imagining things, 5) paranoid, 6) a prude, or 7) a bitch—whatever they can think of to invalidate your feelings as well as your rights to fairness, consideration, and respect, you can remain calm and confident in the truth of your position. It's wise at this moment not to escalate potential conflict, because you want to avoid name-calling, threats, or violence. If the situation heats up, risking your safety despite your most serious efforts, your best option is to remove yourself from the situation—at least for the time being.

On the other hand, the person who's offended you might apologize. Only you can decide whether it's sincere. If it's the first offense, you may give him or her the benefit of the doubt. If that person is a family member, or someone you think you want in your life, it's up to you to reinforce your standards in the future—asserting your boundaries consistently.

The question then becomes: how many times must you say "no," or "that hurts me" before he or she stops the hostile, offensive behavior and treats you with respect? For your own wellbeing, peace of mind, and protection, I hope you won't keep this toxic, predatory person in your life—with license to harm or destroy you on an ongoing basis. It's never worth it.

To emphasize my previous cautionary advice: If you're in a place in your life where others berate or hurt you with impunity, please know that you are an amazing woman—intelligent, kind, and worthy of love and respect. Seek other caring people within your reach who can help you take the steps toward safety and peace of mind in your life. Couples Counseling could help. But if you find yourself a target of someone's violence, The National Sexual Assault Hotline at

1-800-656 HOPE (4673) or the National Domestic Abuse Hotline at 1-800-799-7233. Other local organizations that offer assistance can be found online or through churches and other community resources. Should you decide to leave your situation, keep your plan confidential and learn from professionals how to prepare your escape from a dangerous environment in the safest possible way. If you realize your physical safety is about to be compromised, call 911.

HOW TO REACH OUT

We may already support other women in our hearts and minds, but unless we act on our feelings, we're not really effecting positive change. Reaching out alludes to action. The most positive change we can achieve among women is to strengthen our bonds with one another, thereby making us stronger as individuals, as a group, a community, and ultimately on a global level.

If we each invest the time, energy and compassion to reach out to the women we know, as well as ones we don't know, we're all advancing one another to make a real difference. Here's just one simple way:

- Contact a woman by phone that you haven't talked with in awhile—perhaps she's someone you just met—just to check in and say *hello*.
- Ask if she has a few moments, or if it's a good time to call. She may be busy or on her way out the door. If so, offer to call again.
- If she has time to talk, ask a question that shows you're thinking about her wellbeing. This can be as simple as, "How have you been?"
- Listen to her answers. Don't interrupt her. (This is counter-intuitive, since we're prone to think about our response to someone who's talking, rather than listening to every word she is saying.)
- When she pauses, respond in caring ways to show that you've been listening with empathy. Keep it about her, not you.

- When you respond, refrain from trying to top her story with one that you think is more important or more entertaining. This is not a contest. It's a conversation.
- Keep your comments honest, humble, and brief. It may be OK to talk about an accomplishment but *soft-pedal* it. Be ready to laugh at yourself. Always make her comfort a priority.
- Don't be too anxious to close the conversation. You can afford to take this time to reinforce a connection, making it more meaningful. It's appropriate to ask another question and repeat your initial process.

The benefits of making this call are limitless. Although it may seem to amount to nothing— at least at first—a deeper friendship may grow out of this casual encounter. It not, there's no harm done: At the very least, she will appreciate your effort and may even reciprocate. Nothing needs to be forced or seem unnatural.

Whatever the outcome of this call, you have every reason to feel good about it, because you put the other woman's words and comfort ahead of your own, if only for a few moments. It's likely to feel so good, you'll want to do it again. So you call someone else, strike up a conversation in the grocery store, write a note to a friend, or approach another woman at a meeting or party.

Of course, you can reach out to others every day of the year, as many times as you like. Maybe you already do. If not, you may be surprised how much joy this can create in your life and the lives of others.

Before you know it, you're making genuine friends, expanding your support network, and actively creating new ways to engage with other women—meeting with one another to explore and promote common interests and helping each other advance.

Perhaps you'll want to form an informal group, alliance, business, food bank or any non-profit organization with the purpose to assist women, children and any underserved members of your community in meeting their urgent needs for sustenance, healthcare, and safety, connection and purpose.

SELF-LOVE AND INTEGRITY

THE VALUE OF SELF LOVE

H ave you ever stopped to think about what it means to love yourself? Do you dismiss self-love as being selfish or self-indulgent? Does putting yourself first seem like a direct contradiction to loving others? Do you ever doubt that you're worthy of love? These are matters many of us have questioned, including me.

Often, we hold ourselves to impossible standards in trying to be deserving of others' love as well as our own. In fact, we can be our own worst enemies. In our quest for love and acceptance, we forget that being attractive has more to do with a genuine smile from a loving heart than the result of superficial beauty enhancements. We ignore the fact that another's admiration is more likely in response to our kindness and character than our material belongings—at least it should be.

Here's another conundrum: our efforts to be kind, patient, and loving are sometimes met with indifference. Even worse, our thoughtfulness is taken as weakness and our generosity is considered foolish. We believe we're the nice guys who always finish last. Well, it's time to stop believing our caring attitude may be a waste of time. In truth, coldness and cruelty are never a winning combination—not in the long run.

While underhanded and bullying tactics may work on occasion in crossing a presumed *finish line* first, if we examine more closely their damaging results, we realize that line isn't worth crossing for attention, financial gain, or any conquest that requires we compromise our values. When we consider how to love ourselves without hurting or short-changing others, it can be helpful to substitute the word *love* with the word *value*.

You do a disservice to everyone if you don't learn to value yourself. In order to serve others' as well as your self-interest, it's essential that you become aware of your innate value. By virtue of being human, we're all born with the abilities to love and to reason. These are gifts with tremendous potential value to share with the universe. Disregard for our capacities to extend human decency can do enormous harm to our fellow man. Plus neglect—including self-neglect— has a ripple effect in contaminating humanity.

As you learn to appreciate that your value lies within your unique power to do good, you can make a conscious choice to be a contributing adult who is adding to the collective benefit of society. This is preferable to deciding you're incapable of making a positive difference and remaining passive—leaving a void where you could spread a constructive influence.

Loving yourself is the defining decision to acknowledge your latent power and act consistently according to your highest values, which almost always include integrity and caring for your fellow man. Demonstrating love for others is the epitome of worthiness and the genuine basis for self-love.

BE UNFLAPPABLE, BE UNSTOPPABLE

It seems we're always trying to make sense of all the conflicting advice we hear about dealing with our emotions. We're told to honor our feelings—to own them. We expect others to validate our feelings. If they're ignored or dismissed, we consider it a serious transgression, such as abuse.

Beyond this, we're advised to be assertive whenever we communicate what we want. Assertiveness is generally acknowledged to be a better tactic than aggressiveness in responding to rude behavior, bullying, abuse or neglect. But the circumstances of any human interaction are open to question, since they involve more than one point of view. Others with different perspectives may see us as selfish or self-righteous in demanding we get our way—no matter whether we use polite or harsh means.

The issue of *political correctness*—the avoidance of words or actions perceived to marginalize, exclude, or insult others, especially those who are disadvantaged or discriminated against— hovers at the top of the list of acceptable behaviors we must observe to avoid offending others. Especially in our litigious culture, almost anything we say could cause costly offense.

Emotions are often complicated and tough to analyze. What might cause great offense or emotional pain to one person doesn't even show on the sensitivity radar for another. Besides, life comes at us fast. Many of us struggle to say afloat, and don't have the luxury to examine all the feelings we experience in an hour—not to mention on a daily basis.

In solving this enigma, it helps to approach life with calmness despite all the offenses—many of them petty—that we continually endure. Composure is effective and energy saving. We simply don't have the time or the strength to fight every potential conflict that's thrown our way. When we're constantly trying to defend our *rightful* positions, we end up emotionally exhausted and depleted of our power to move forward. Every time we stop to address a small offense to our sensibilities, we're interrupting our advancement as self-contained and gracious human beings.

Especially as women, we've developed a keen awareness of the words and actions of those in our sphere of influence. Our instincts guide us to protect the honor and safety of our loved ones—often even before our own. But it's not in our best interests to act in response to every single breach of our standards, especially when it slows our progress in achieving beneficial results toward a larger purpose. At the same time, we don't want to be viewed as *doormats*. Often, just the right look or a moment of silence can be most efficient in warding off ill-intentioned acts or remarks.

If someone or something is repeatedly threatening your dignity or wellbeing, you can avert your knee-jerk reaction by postponing a discussion to a more appropriate time, when the parties involved are likely to be more rational and calm than in the *heat of battle*. In maneuvering through this quagmire we call life, try to think of yourself as an Olympic skater gliding gracefully through potential hazards like snow and cracks on the ice in order to complete a near-flawless performance, rather than a distraught single mom driving a car that's stuck in traffic and honking in futility because you can't move. That's just one scenario. I'm sure you can think of more.

Your poise and capacity for understanding in difficult situations will earn you more respect and admiration than exposing a defensive attitude every time your patience is challenged. Just as important, the consistent practice of presenting your most upbeat and unflappable presence will help lead you to your priceless peace of mind!

Further the calm self-assurance you cultivate will greatly assist you in reaching your ultimate destination in your quest for self-actualization and a life made meaningful with love.

SHINE YOUR INNER LIGHT

In everyday life, letting your inner light beam with observable *voltage* is of vital significance in all your relationships. Your attitude determines the impression you make on others—often before you say a word. With surprising accuracy, almost anyone can pick up on your energy level and desire to connect through your speaking inflections, facial expressions and body language. Project the power of your light from your very soul.

When you learn to develop a prevailing attitude that shines, you can uncover vast new opportunities for the realization of your desires, needs and objectives. Your *can do* confidence signals your availability, openness and connectedness to the universe. Whether it's intentional or not, an important aspect of your personality revealed by your attitude is your self-esteem. When you learn to love yourself you feel more confident to open yourself to others and convey your inner happiness with a characteristic glow. To transmit your *highest voltage* requires your brightest shine.

And yet many of us have experienced some sort of sabotage to damage our self-concept. We aren't all born into perfect families. Even loving parents may undermine our self-image with negative outlooks, unrealistic expectations, comparisons to siblings, or lack of understanding and attention. In school, bullying is a universal issue.

When we graduate from high school or college with hopes of conquering the world, our well-meaning dreams can be shattered— at least on our first try to make a positive and powerful impact. We need strength to pull together and try again to achieve any amount of success on our terms. This can require a little *lightening up*—instead of stressful overthinking—in order to radiate our confidence in our ability to overcome challenges.

Sometimes the simplest and most effective action we can take in adapting to the ordeals we face is to smile. Some may think *that's too easy, it doesn't solve anything* or *it's manipulative.* I've heard women claiming that they resent it when others—in particular men—tell them to smile. While none of us like to be told what to do or how to present ourselves, we also seem to have an aversion to smiling, because we don't want to appear submissive or seem like we're trying to win others' approval. This is understandable. It harkens back to our history of discrimination—including the days when we were told to "love, honor and *obey*" our husbands.

Instead of reverting to survival modes we established in the past, today we can assume our equal status with men. A smile can signify our comfort within our own skin. It can be inviting, startling, and blindingly beautiful on a woman's countenance—especially when it's authentic and comes deep from within. Granted, when we first practice smiling as a way of communicating to others that we're self-assured, it may not feel natural. But it becomes more genuine as we notice others smiling back at us. When a relationship starts with a mutual smile, it has a real chance of leading into a conversation that's enjoyable and productive for both parties.

As an alternative to resisting any mannerisms that you think might make you appear vulnerable you can practice buffing your shine to a warm and steady glow. The paradox is that when you let yourself be real and acknowledge your humanity with an acquiescent smile, you actually grow in strength. Love requires courage—a welcome alternative to fear.

It's helpful to practice radiating your unique voltage on an unwavering basis, because your *current* needs to be strong enough to withstand any efforts to dim your light. While you may not be a believer at first, you can test my theories any time and in any circumstance. If the person receiving your glowing warmth remains grim-faced, don't take it personally. Just repeat the word *next* in your mind and move on. The glowing radiance on the faces of the men and women responding to yours with enthusiasm and appreciation will far outshine any trifling rejections.

Besides, despite any possible outcome, projecting a genuine air of warmth and friendliness will make you feel fantastic from within.

To Empower Yourself Walk Your Talk

A woman who walks her talk is a woman whose words are consistent with her actions. She's honest, she's real, and she has integrity; in other words, she's *authentic*. Her credibility is her most valuable strength as an effective communicator: she understands that her actions are more important in communicating who she is than her words.

The familiar phrase, "Actions speak louder than words," is one of the most profound observations about human behavior. All actions are in fact considered *nonverbal communication*. Without exception, our actions are our most powerful means of communicating with others.

Until we back our *talk* with action, our words are open to question. It isn't what we say or think that defines us, but what we do. In fairness, both women and men have sometimes been found to lack in credibility.

As women in particular, we may complain that no one takes us seriously. Sometimes we experience a dismissive or patronizing attitude when we don't deserve it. It may be based on an unfair bias that *women are the weaker sex* or some other demeaning assumption. Before we open our mouths or take a step forward, we face an image problem based on unjust stereotypes. We must counteract them if we want to advance.

To neutralize this prevalent form of discrimination, it's paramount that we apply our standards with irrefutable force. In other words, when women say something we'd better mean it, and—even more important—we'd better prove that we mean what we say with our responsible actions. The eyes of the world are upon us and many are judging our every step—often with distrust, cynicism, and misogynistic attitudes.

Men have credibility issues too. Ironically, as opposed to our presumed lack of reliability as objects of discrimination, any doubts about men's honesty are more likely based on their position of privilege. The phrase *a man is as good as his word* applies to business agreements in which its importance is acknowledged but not always observed. When it comes to romance or domestic relationships, countless examples reinforce the fact that men can take concepts of honesty and commitment lightly.

As an illustration, there's an axiom that *women fall in love with their ears, men with their eyes.* This suggests that a woman will believe the flattering words any man may use when he's trying to win her over. The words may or may not be true. But if a man is literally *sweeping you off your feet* with his charm, here's a word of advice: A smart woman doesn't believe everything she hears: she lets a man's actions speak for him, not his words.

If women want to gain credibility, respect and validity, we must be accountable for our actions. If we promise something and don't deliver, regardless how much we apologize, our words are meaningless. It's not until we follow through on our verbal assurances that we're considered believable and worthy of trust.

To take it a step further, "Actions may speak louder than words, but intentions speak the loudest." If you're making a statement about your intentions that your actions have already proven false, your lack of sincerity will be the only thing that rings loud and true.

Beyond this, even your best intentions won't mean much if you haven't even begun to take any action. Procrastinating is not a sufficient excuse for not actualizing your words. In fact, no excuse will suffice. If you want something enough, you'll find a way to accomplish it.

We're always responsible for our actions, no matter how we feel: As an example with universal implications, authentic love isn't only a feeling; it's an action that demonstrates and verifies our love on a reliable basis.

WOMEN AND GRATITUDE

Gratitude or thankfulness is an attitude that actually creates joy when we practice it. Gratitude has little to do with how many material things we own and everything to do with our humbleness and appreciation for what we have, which is best measured by intangible blessings. Gratitude may sometimes make a deeper emotional impact among people who have little financial comfort than on those privileged to have many luxuries and few worries about basic things like safety, shelter, food and warmth.

Those of us who have more than enough creature comforts without struggling to attain them can tend to take our advantages for granted. We may begin to feel entitled to everything, according to our *birthright*. At the opposite end of the spectrum, many of us find it a constant challenge to provide for our basic needs, but gratitude helps us transcend our sense of scarcity and fill the emptiness with feelings of abundance and happiness.

When you practice gratitude in your daily life, you begin to feel better inside. In expressing your gratitude to loved ones, friends, and virtual strangers—for making the effort to enhance your life experience—you transform their generosity into the mutual sharing of joy.

Gratitude determines our humanity and raises us above our baser inclinations of doing whatever will serve our vanity and greed, regardless of whether our selfish actions hurt or even destroy others *in our way.*

While women are unequivocally equal to men, millions of us are trying to advance in achieving financial independence. As part of this process, we're demanding equal pay for equal work. We may question the effectiveness of gratitude in gaining our autonomy. We feel we have the right to succeed on our own merit, but at the same time we owe a debt of gratitude to any man who helps provide for our economic survival as a sponsor, mentor, boss, father, husband or friend. Understandably we might be conflicted about our appropriate roles in their lives and theirs in ours.

We don't want to be meek, submissive, and subservient. We may carry feelings of resentment toward those we perceive as holding us back. We become angry whenever our needs aren't met. While our wrath is sometimes justifiable, it's rarely effective in accomplishing our objectives. Every time we vent our anger and place blame, we're likely damaging our relationships with those who care about us and have the capacity to help us. In other words, we're antagonizing those with influence—usually men.

When we project an obstinate attitude, any progress we may seem to make that emanates from rage and indignation is an illusion since it doesn't include acknowledgement of some degree of dependence on those who have largely controlled our fate. Real advancement is contingent on the expression of our gratitude for what we have, not our aversion for that which we don't have in our personal and business lives.

The forum where we can best express our entitlement to human rights is politics—local, state and national. In fact, it's our responsibility to express to our government what we believe is unfair. Through campaigning, voting, and assuming leadership positions, we stand the greatest chance to gain the liberties we deserve. It's a tough fight, but we're proving that we're up to it.

Historically, women have earned particular respect for our compassion. Some men—and women—consider it a weakness, but arguably it's our greatest strength. Our consistent demonstration of love, including our expression of gratitude—even in the most challenging and painful circumstances—greatly defines our characters. We would be unwise to ignore or compromise our remarkable gift.

Within the context of our loving and respectful gratitude, our words of justifiable anger will more likely be accepted, acknowledged, and answered with emerging regard and effort to meet our needs.

TAKE THE HIGH ROAD
TO HAPPINESS

I n our vast universe, there are as many roads to happiness as people who are seeking it. No two roads are alike just as each of us is unique. None of us can judge another individual's choices regarding the way to find it.

However, we can explore what happiness is and how we might achieve it. Although we are each one-of-a-kind, human beings share a common connection or *oneness*. While our emotional makeup may vary, we smile when something brings us joy, we laugh when we're amused, we cry when we lose a loved one, and we're angry when we're betrayed.

I become concerned when I read that our greatest and likely our only goal is happiness. While it's certainly true that happiness can help provide us with the strength to act on our own behalf or for the good of others, it's largely a by-product of our actions, not the ultimate goal. Besides, it's little like the chicken or the egg puzzle: Which comes first—happiness or action? We can examine two concepts: 1) What actions can make us happy? 2) Are actions necessary for happiness?

Happiness doesn't depend on outside circumstances, but rather a state of mind we must cultivate unless we have the rare good fortune to be born with a happy disposition that we maintain throughout our lives. While pre-packaged happiness may be possible with some exceptional DNA, our environment probably has the greatest effect on the state of our emotions. Most of us need practice creating happiness within ourselves through 1) caring for others, which depends on—and engenders—our self-worth and 2) self-care based on self-love, which is necessary to refuel and refresh us, in order to share our love with loved ones, friends and everyone who benefits from our actions.

We often measure our happiness by our accomplishments. We may consider marriage, raising a family, and holding down a job or career among our achievements. While these may be conventional rungs on the *ladder to success*, they don't necessarily lead to happiness. They might be noble pursuits, but they're relatively meaningless unless we prioritize our open expression of love and compassion for others in achieving these goals.

Someone may think that he or she can find happiness in quantifiable *success*. Perhaps without learning the value of money or the obligation to be accountable for his or her actions, this individual might feel entitled to all the material symbols of success: an Ivy League education, marriage into a wealthy family, world travel, expensive cars, designer clothes—the whole package. I venture to say that these attractive perks may bring some semblance of happiness—and let's face it, feelings of pleasure many of us dream of, especially during our moments of frustration—but the potential for joy is missing when greed takes precedence over love.

Calculable measures of success do not determine happiness. Not all of us are born with the means to afford even the simplest luxuries of life. Some of us struggle to provide ourselves with the most basic necessities. Job training or education is not always available or affordable. Even food is in short supply. Without the means of self-support—not to mention the resources to support a family—the only option is to strive hard to provide for the basic means of survival.

But there's reason for optimism: Remarkably, many who are born into humble surroundings and left without apparent means still seem to possess an invisible source of happiness and gratitude that doesn't depend on material advantages. Despite hardships, they show a great capacity for generosity. These courageous members of humanity deserve respect.

If we are fortunate to enjoy more advantages than others in our community or anywhere on the globe, time we can spare out of our busy lives to help our underserved neighbors begin to help themselves will not only uplift them, it can also bring us pleasure, peace of mind, and satisfaction for our efforts—perhaps more than we might experience from fleeting self-gratification, such as purchasing luxury items we don't need.

Sure, some self-indulgence is a good thing. Plan that big vacation. Delight in the double-chocolate lava cake. Put up your feet and enjoy a glass of wine. Travel to Europe. Take a long nap. Do what it takes to make you feel good and energize you for another week of work in a job you took to pay the bills while you plan for that dream career a few years ahead. Maybe you don't have the time or the means to plan beyond tomorrow. Treat yourself, at least once in while, to the little things that will make you feel content. But only use *things* as a fallback solution for creating happiness. Keep top-of-mind that your primary source of happiness is experiencing love and sharing it with others.

Individual happiness is subjective and mysterious, based on unseen layers of our capacity and potential for love and little or nothing to do with material wealth or prestige. Someone who puts others first may even transcend happiness and find something deeper we call joy. An enigma of life is that although the human race exhibits inestimable diversity, at the same time we are all one. Although happiness and joy originates from within ourselves, we need one another to embrace it and thus enhance it together.

We would all be shallow indeed if our only goal was to live in a constant state of happiness without any investment of love. As we evolve, we realize love is often a conscious choice. It's more of a verb than a noun—something we do, not just something we feel. As human beings, in order to grow we must develop our potential for good. Happiness and its deepest manifestation joy emanate from our victory over the more selfish side of our natures. The countless roads that lead us each to happiness beckon us to love something larger than ourselves and share our awareness as we evolve together.

Printed in the United States
By Bookmasters